DRAWING THE SAMURAI SWORD

"Spirit" calligraphy by Iwao Bokai

DRAWING THE SAMURAI SWORD

THE JAPANESE ART OF SWORDSMANSHIP

居合

Darrell Max Craig

TUTTLE Publishing

Tokyo | Rutland, Vermont | Singapore

Published by Tuttle Publishing, an imprint of Periplus Editions (HK) Ltd.

www.tuttlepublishing.com

Copyright © 1981, 1988, 2018 Darrell Max Craig
Cover photo by kkong5/iStockphoto.com

Library of Congress Cataloging-in-Publication Data: 83-193519

First published in 1981 by Lotus Press Ltd., Chofu P.O. Box 15, Chofu-shi, Tokyo 182-91 Japan
Previously published as *IAI-Jitsu: Center of the Circle*

ISBN 978-0-8048-5008-7

Distributed by:

North America, Latin America & Europe
Tuttle Publishing
364 Innovation Drive, North Clarendon
VT 05759-9436 U.S.A.
Tel: (802) 773-8930
Fax: (802) 773-6993
info@tuttlepublishing.com
www.tuttlepublishing.com

Asia Pacific
Berkeley Books Pte. Ltd.
 3 Kallang Sector #04-01
Singapore 349278
Tel: (65) 6741-2178
Fax: (65) 6741-2179
inquiries@periplus.com.sg
www.tuttlepublishing.com

Japan
Tuttle Publishing
Yaekari Building, 3rd Floor
5-4-12 Osaki, Shinagawa-ku
Tokyo 141 0032
Tel: (81) 3 5437-0171
Fax: (81) 3 5437-0755
sales@tuttle.co.jp
www.tuttle.co.jp

Second Edition
26 25 24 23 22   65 4 3 2   2205TP

Printed in Singapore

TUTTLE PUBLISHING® is a registered trademark of Tuttle Publishing, a division of Periplus Editions (HK) Ltd.

Acknowledgments

I wish to express my sincere appreciation to my wife, Mary Ann Craig, for her patience and for her word processing. Also to:

Mrs. Violet Clark, for her time;

Mr. Terry Burge, for editing;

Mrs. Mary Schultz and Mr. Mark Hunter, for illustrations;

Mr. Joseph L. Rachel, for photography;

Ms. Pat Metcalf Bissonnet, for assistance with this new edition.

Without their help, this book would only be half-finished.

Author Darrell Max Craig—Kesagiri kata

Contents

This book is dedicated to the memory of Sensei Harutane Chiba of the Hokushin style of Kendo in Osaka, Japan

Spiritual guidance between Buddhist priest, Sobojo, and a Samurai warrior,
by Ushiwakamaru.

Author's Preface

 I feel that every man or woman on this earth has something to contribute to the subject that they love, and I can say without remorse that I have an ongoing love affair with the Japanese Sword. Chiba Sensei told me years ago that when you practice Batto—the original term for drawing the sword—or any sword arts, you must have *ki, ken,* and *tai,* meaning spirit, sword, and body. When put together, these three things make an immovable mountain.

This book will not be the answer to all your questions, but I hope it will answer some. Most Japanese senseis of Iaido or Batto concede that Hayashizaki Jinsuke Shigenobu was the creative genius and founder of Iaido, or, "drawing of the sword." Starting about 450 years ago, this tradition has been passed from generation to generation. Shigenobu regulated Batto as an independent art and named it Shigenobu-Ryu or Hayashizaki-Ryu. Since it began, the art "meaning of Batto" has thrived within a great number of traditional dojos in Japan. A student could study his whole life and still not master all of these old *ryu-ha,* or old styles. Consequently, the All Japan Kendo Association—now the All Japan Kendo Remmei—established what is called Seitei-Gata Iaido. The Japan Remmei commissioned eleven *hanshi dan* (master swordsmen) to unite techniques from different ryu-ha into a system suitable for beginning students. This board completed their study in 1968 and selected seven katas suitable for the beginning student. In 1977 the Remmei added three additional katas. These were all *tachi-iai-no-bu,* or standing katas. They are not included in this edition.

I feel that the seven katas of Seitei-Gata included in this book contain ninety percent of the fundamentals that are needed to perfect one's practice. The students of Iaido should always keep in mind that the kata Ippon Me Mae is considered among most senseis to be the most important. It has all the basic fundamentals of Iaido or Batto. Most old ryu-ha have this kata in their system in some form.

Iaido consists of four movements: (1) *nukitsuke,* or draw (2) *kiritsuke,* or cutting movements (3) *chiburi,* or removing the blood from the sword, and (4) *noto,* or return of the sword to its *saya* or scabbard. After the development of Iaido, some 400 different ryu-has were officially cataloged in Japan. The three styles we are concerned with here: (1) All Japan Kendo Remmei, (2) Mu-gai-Hyodo-Ryu of Tsji Gettan Sukemochi—where there are five different *sokes* (presidents). In Japan the style of Mu-gai-Ryu I am familiar with is that of Ishii Gogetsu (Soke) of Sakai City, Japan, and (3) Chiba Hokushin Ito-Ryu. Although the Japan Remmei Iaido is made up of different old ryu-has, I feel it may be beneficial for the student to be familiar with two other old ryu-has. I have included in this edition several different wazas from Mu-gai-Ryu, one two-man kata from Hokushin Ito-Ryu, and several human body test cuts that were performed at the Kozukabara Execution Grounds in Edo before the Meiji Restoration.

Harutane Chiba Sensei once told me that a person who studies the way of the sword must also study Bushido. He must bear in mind his moral duty. He must have a good heart and he must have faith. These are like the two wheels of a *jinrikisha* ("rickshaw"). This is the very heart of Bushido, the Way of the Warrior. The word Bushido and Samarai (Bushi) go hand-in-hand. Bushido means the way of the Bushi.

The professional military men of Japan rose as a distinct class in the twelfth century. In the thirteenth century they successfully defended Japan against Kublai Khan's Mongol invasion forces. Amazingly enough, the Japanese warrior did not overpower Kubili Khan's forces—the Mongols were decimated by an unexpected typhoon. A similar incident happened several years later when another typhoon saved the Japanese from a war with Kublai Khan's forces. The Samurai considered this a gift from the gods and called it *kama kazi*, or "divine wind." Unfortunately, after this high point, inter-clan fighting undermined the Samurai class.

The new National Unification brought all of this to an end in 1603, by way of the Tokugawa family, which ruled Japan with an iron hand until 1867. In 1868, under the rule of Emperor Meiji, feudalism was abolished. It is important to note here that even though feudalism had been abolished, Bushido lived on. The way of the warrior was supposed to be concerned with the inner workings of the spirit of the Samurai. Bushido has much in common with the concept of chivalry in the West. A Samarai was supposed to be a warrior of kindness and respectability as well as exemplifying physical and moral courage. Like the chivalry of Western Europe, Bushido left a legacy founded on an unwritten code of distinction; rooted in consideration for the weak, and backed by moral courage. This unwritten code for Western European gentlemen has mostly passed away with time, though it left a general respect for honesty, kindness and courage.

There are basically two types of Samarai swords, the katana and the *tachi*. The term "tachi" refers to the sword's mountings, meaning they are hung from the belt on the Samarai amour with the cutting edge facing down—a style favored by higher ranked Samarai on horseback. In the fourteenth century, a new type of sword was developed; the *katana*—23½ to 28½ inches in blade length. The katana was mounted to be worn with the cutting edge facing up in the Samurai's *obi* (belt). This type of sword became the weapon of choice for lower-ranking individuals who needed a sword more suitable to their changing battle conditions. The katana, with its curvature near the *kissaki* (end), offered the combatant a faster response time, allowing the sword to be drawn with a cutting action in a single motion. For the Samarai, the outward sign of rank was the *daisho*, literally, "big and small." The "big" was the katana, and the "small" blade was the *wakizashi*, about 20 inches in length. To use both swords at the same time was referred to as Nito-Ryu, and was made famous by Miyamoto Musashi (1584–1645).

When indoors, the katana was removed from the obi and placed on a rack at the entrance. On the battlefield, it was customary to carry the katana and a more practical short dagger called a *tanto* (6–12 inches). These swords and daggers are extremely collectible, being produced by expert craftsman who have become unsurpassed in the artistic expression of lethal beauty.

Blades forged before 1596 are called *koto* or "old swords." Those after 1596 are considered "new swords" (*shinto*), and those that were made in the nineteenth century or later or referred to as *shin-shinto* ("new-new swords"). The main characteristics of a Japanese sword is the appearance of a tempering pattern along the cutting edge called *hamon*, and it can appear in a wide range of configurations—see page 21. On the other hand, if one looks at history's established record, the Samarai sword as we have come to know it is the only sword that was used as a weapon of destruction by a population until as late as 1945. That was only about 70 years ago!

After 1945, the Japanese sword moved into history and the minds and imaginations of people all over the globe. In today's world, we associate this piece of Japanese history with the martial arts known as Iaido, Batto-Jitsu, or Kendo. Iaido and Batto are arts of the sword that involve a quick draw to slash the opponent. Kendo, on the other hand, refers to "the way of the sword," *ken* meaning "sword," and *do* meaning "way." Before the word Kendo became widespread it had numerous names, such as Tojutsu, Toho, Tachiuchi, and the most commonly used term; Kenjitsu.

I have been practicing Budo for fifty years. In this time frame I have been asked the question many times, "which art is the best, Kendo or Iaido?" To me (and every sensei I have put this question to), the answer has always been the same; they are inseparable. The cutting actions of Iaido and Kendo have the same Japanese *ma-ai* (engagement distance): (1) Three-step distance, (2) Two-step distance, and (3—most important) One-step distance. Although these three distances are the same for both arts, I find it difficult for the Iai student to properly achieve the distances with an imaginary opponent. With Kendo or two-person katas included in the practice, the distance is no longer imaginary. This is one reason I feel the kata Ippon Me Mae is so important. Not only does the kata allow the student to find the distance of Issoku-Itto-No-Ma-Ai, a one-step interval; it also allows the student to find the second step interval. It brings the body and sword into harmony with the explosive *kiai* with the first cut to the attacker's right temple, followed by a natural downward cut in the second step.

Needless to say, it makes no sense to argue for the preservation of the martial arts or its traditions. I believe in judging the merit of Kendo and Iaido from an open standpoint, evaluating its worth to the individual and society. You can sum this up in one simple question; "Will the understanding of the art benefit me more that just copying a set of mechanical motions?" If the answer is yes, then the decision that one must make is self-evident.

Although some people have called Iaido a religion, I find this hard to accept. However, I must also point out that though I do not consider it to be a religion, it is so interwoven with certain religious beliefs that they are inseparable; I have never entered a Japanese dojo that did not have a Shinto shrine. Iaido is a result of generations of development in Japan, and while the West uses it for self-expression, the Japanese use it for mind improvement. Thus, while the outward body of movements may be the same, the difference in attitude is great. Where mere technical knowledge is not enough to master Iaido, you must go deeply into the inner spirit of the art. Training in Iaido can only be successful when you have absorbed the mental as well as the physical techniques so that they are so much a part of you that using them is purely intuitive and subconscious. Your attitude should be one of alertness mixed with calmness and fearlessness.

When practicing Iaido you must create a consciousness free from all thoughts, reflections, or distractions of any kind. The sword must become as much a part of you as your leg is; when you do something, it just moves without thought. When picking up a sword you should handle it as an extension of your arm. When you can do Iai as if you were eating, without stopping for your brain to tell you each individual motion needed to move the spoon into your mouth, then it is natural. "You are said to have mastered the art when the technique works through your body and limbs as if independent of your conscious mind."[1]

---

[1]   D. T. Suzuki, *Zen and Japanese Culture.* Princeton, NJ: Princeton University Press, 1971. p. 74

BEGINNER'S MIND: "In the beginner's mind there are many possibilities, but in the expert's there are few."

The characters for "beginner's" mind, brushed by Darrell Craig.

Zen Mind, Beginner's Mind by Shunryu Suzuki

Muramatsu Kibei Hidenao (ronin of Ako)

CHAPTER ONE

Examining and Sword Servicing

And when the swordsmith handed it to me:

> All who beheld it said a long and whispered "Ahhh" at the strip of silver steel made with love and skill for the single purpose of opening live human flesh.[1]

I knew it was mine and when I learned all there was to know about it, it became me, and I became it. It gave me the soul I was searching for, and I gave it the heart to come alive. Together we saved many lives.

> For the Japanese the sword is more than just a weapon. It has mysterious powers like the cross to the Christians. It is felt that the sword receives its "soul" from the swordsmith during the forging and tempering process. It is for this reason that swordsmiths were treated with respect equal to, if not greater than, that given a priest.[2]

The entire manufacturing process was a ritual that began with the swordsmith fasting and making prayers to the god of his forge and ended with the quenching of the sword in a manner learned through many years of work and study.

The swordsmith, through the strength and charity of his efforts, is felt to take part of his soul, blend it with energy from the gods and this becomes the soul of the sword. Each sword is felt to reflect the true "Self" of its maker.

> As something of divinity enters into the making of the sword, its owner and user ought also to respond to the inspiration. He ought to be a spiritual man, not an agent of brutality.[3]

The nomenclature of a sword is simple in some aspects and complex in others. I am by no means an expert in the science of swords. This I leave to men in that field. My contribution is to let the people who have a Japanese sword know a little something about it, and, if they are interested, to learn an art with it. As you can see by the drawings on the following pages, swords have many different *tangs* or ends that go under the wooden handle. This part of the blade is where the date and signature are found. One must remember; just because the tang does not have a signature or a date, does not mean that it is not valuable. You could have a very old date and maker's name on the tang and it may be worthless. On the other hand, an unsigned tang could be worth a small fortune.

---

[1] W. D. Jennings, *The Ronin*. Rutland, VT: Charles E. Tuttle Co., 1968. p. 129
[2] Rodger Fitlock, "Japanese Cross," *Black Belt Magazine*, 7~5. May, 1969. p. 49
[3] D. T. Suzuki, *Zen and Japanese Culture* Princeton, NJ: Princeton University Press, 1971. p. 93

Fig. 1

Fig. 1A

Cap-Kojiri

Saya-Scabbard

Kurikata-Cord Knob

Shitotome

Kogai and Kozuka-Pockets

Washers-Seppa

Tsuba-Guard

Kozuka-Utility Knife

Kogai-Skewer

Mekugi-Pin

Same-ray Skin

Kashira

Tsuka-Handle

Tsukaito-makidome-hilt-knot

Fuchi-Sleeve

Tsuka ito-cord

Menuki-Ornament

Kizu—Flaws

Karasuguchi
Crow beak crack of tip

Tsukinowa
Crescent shape crack
not touching edge

Kitaware
Forging cracks

Muneshinae
Wrinkles on back

Hashinae
Cutting edge wrinkles

Tsugishinae
Bent cracks

Muneware
Lengthwise crack
in back

Hagire
Cross-Wise cracks

Hagarami
Diagonal Crack

Tateware
Lengthwise crack

Tobishimi
Spatter stains

Mukade shinae
Centipede wrinkles

Yakikuzure
Broken temper line

Shimi
Dark stains

Fukure
Air pockets

Hasamidashi
Cutting edge cracks

Jiare
Blisters

Sumi gomori
Carbon pockets

Umeqane
Filled holes

Points

Wide groove on one side of shinogi

Tip stops short of shinogi end

Round end groove

Sloping end of groove

Square end groove

File Marks

Tang-File Marks

Hidari sujikai
Reverse oblique

Sujikai
Regular oblique

Decorative patterns

Higaki
Criss-cross

Reverse
Takanoha

Katesagari

Sensuki
Draw-shave marks

Takanoha
Hawk feather

Katesagari
Slightly down

Slightly up to right

Yokayasuri
Horizontal

Tsuchime
Hammer marks

Midare
Uneven marks

Hirakiri shinogi
sujikai-Horizontal
surface, oblique shinogi

Hirasujikai-oblique
surface, straight on
shinogi

Tangs

Tang Ends

Nakago-Tangs

Katsugi
Sliced side

Kurijri
Chestnut

Furisode
Sleeve

Tanago
Fish belly

Kiri-Square

Kengyo-Pointed

Shirihari
Wide base

Futsu-Normal

Tanago-Extreme
Fish belly

Hagari
Left side up

Katayama-Kengyo
Pointed

Funasoko
Ship bottom

Goheigata-Shinto
paper symbol shape

Kijimata
Pheasant tail

Fig. 2

Yakiba—Temper Lines

Minigata—Ear shape patterns

Midare with ears, islands and jewels

Full temper

Full temper

Large midare with tobiyaki lines—about half full temper

Uma-no-ha—Horse teeth pattern

Large gonome

Juzuba—Priest's beads gonome

Inverted or points up gonome

Kataochi—Drooping shoulder gonome

Gonome midare of scattered nie

Choji midare—Uneven choji

Kobushigata—First shape choji

Slanted choji midare

Choji-midare with asni, leaves and gems

Notare with slanted choji clusters

Shallow notare

Notare—Short waves

Long notare

Toran—High waves

Toran aranami—High breaking waves with spray

Deep gully wavy gonome

Hako—Box pattern

Kuzure—Crumbled line

Nokogiri—Saw tooth midare with ashi

Medium Suguba

Medium suguba of nie with nioi line down the center

Hakkake—Swept line especially at the point

Komidare—Small irregular patterns

Nokogiri midare—Saw teeth somewhat irregular

Midare of scattered nie with ashi and eyes

Saka nokojiri midare—Slanted irregular saw teeth

Sanbonsugi—Three cedar trees

Reverse sanbonsugi with kibaba—demon tangs

Large midare

Mountain peaks and muneyaki (temper along back edge)

Notare midare—Wavy irregular of dense nie

Arrow notch of nioi and nie

Fig. 2A

Tangs with mei and Testing Certification

Tsuba with mei
Fig. 2B

Please let me interject this small note: just because you have a Japanese sword, do not let me make you think that you necessarily have an heirloom. I must also point out that there are a lot of Japanese swords just lying around in garages or attics from World War II that are waiting to be found.

Let me tell you about a friend of mine that I will call Mr. Goodnow. As he and I became better acquainted he started taking up the martial arts from me and he was telling a friend of his about me, Iaido, swords, and one thing and another. This friend one day went to his grandfather's farm out in the country, and there in the barn in the corner were two Japanese swords. Now not knowing anything about them, but remembering what Mr. Goodnow had said, he brought them back to town for me to examine. The thing I would like to point out here is that no one had touched those swords since 1945. They were out there all that time, by some miracle in a dry place, leaning up against a post with a rat's nest at the bottom. When I pulled the blades out of the scabbard, we were all shocked at their mirror-like finish. Not one piece of rust anyplace. Nervously, I pulled off the handles. One proved to be worth about eight hundred dollars and the other worth a couple of hundred dollars. You never know exactly what you have until you examine it thoroughly and get an expert's opinion.

Never, and I repeat never, put your fingers on the blade. The blade is made up of five parts, the *shinogi* (back side one half the way down from the handle), the *hamon* (temper pattern along the cutting edge), the *mune* (back side about 8 inches back from the end), the *monouchi* (first 8 inches of the cutting edge), and the *kissaki* (tip). *(See Figure 1.)* There are two reasons for not touching the blade. First and most important, the *ha* or cutting edge, being of surgical sharpness, will cut you. Secondly, moisture and acids in one's hands will begin to make it rust in a matter of minutes. Take a clean piece of soft paper or cloth and hold the back side while you are looking at it. Look for *kizu*, or flaws. *(See Figure 2.)* Next, look at the hamon, this can be very exciting since there are so many different patterns, and the workmanship is so beautiful. The kissaki is the last thing you should examine. If you hold the sword in the light, it will bring out the beauty even more. Never attempt to sharpen or polish the blade. The Japanese use a series of fine stones to sharpen and bring out the grain of the steel which could be forever lost by inexperienced buffing. If there are small rust spots, they can be removed by using some coarse paper (not sand paper). Something else that I have found helpful to bring out the luster of the blade is silver polish.

There are many types of Japanese swords and not all are the long katanas which we usually think about. For instance, we have the *tachi* (slung sword). *dai katana* (horse sword), standard Samurai katana, *wakizashi* (short sword), *tanto* (dagger), *aikuchi* (dagger without *tsuba*), and the *heyazashi* (a small tanto carried in the clothing). All of these blades had a specific purpose and should be handled with the same care as the katana. *(See Figure 3.)*

If you are looking for a Samurai sword to buy or have one to sell, let me give you a word of warning. You should be careful. It is always better to buy from a known collector rather than from a dealer. Here again, it depends on the quality of blade that you wish to buy or to sell. I think that it is safe to say that the worth of the blade is highly subjective and may be only determined by the person who is buying or selling it. But remember, a collector usually collects quality and a dealer buys and sells only for a living. Many times dealers make a very good living off of the unknowing customers.

I have noticed in the past few years that at gun shows, the Samurai swords for sale have gone down in quality and up in price. This is contributed to by two factors: First, many swords are disappearing, and secondly, blades are being sold back and forth from dealer to dealer.

I know that in this part of the country, since the martial arts boom, many who have taken up a martial art have wanted to own a Samurai sword. This has boosted the price of a twenty dollar sword to about one hundred dollars. The person who knows a little about the swords would not want that kind of a blade. However, some enthusiasts simply have to possess one, no matter what the quality. For instance, a dealer whom I know told me last year that he would buy all the "junk" blades that I could get my hands on. He said, "These kids are buying up things we could not have given away last year at more than a hundred bucks each and we are making a killing."

Let us look at what makes a little better than average katana. First, it should be around 31¾ inches in length (from the *hamachi* or edge notch to the kissaki or point). *(See Figure 1.)* Next, look under the handle at the tang. Slide back the *habaki* or scabbard sleeve and look for a small cherry blossom stamp. If it is there, then you know at once that it is a new blade and made sometime during the Showa era (1926 to present). I once heard a dealer tell a prospective customer to look at all the matching numbers on the blade and on the hardware.

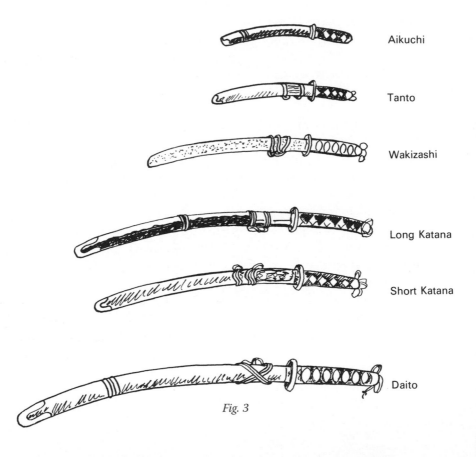

Aikuchi

Tanto

Wakizashi

Long Katana

Short Katana

Daito

Fig. 3

Fig. 4

"That makes this a collectors' item." The customer bought the sword for three hundred dollars. Last year the dealer would have been lucky to get fifteen dollars for it. Remember that doing business at a large gun show is like buying a used car from Crazy Harry's Used Car Lot. Crazy Harry is crazy like a fox.

If you are only going to invest a minimum amount, say seventy-five or one hundred dollars, do not expect to get much for your money. Try to get a blade without too many pits or chips. If possible, get a sword with a wooden saya, no matter what shape it is in; you can always repair it or have it repaired for a minimal cost. The blade is what you are most concerned with. If it is clean, not too heavy, and most importantly—if you can afford it—buy it. If you buy too expensive a sword to begin with, you might damage it while you are beginning to learn Iaido. If you are going to invest several hundred dollars in a sword, I suggest that you either find someone who knows about swords or that you try to read as much as possible about them. There are several good books on Japanese swords in English. Your local library probably has many of these books or you can buy them. Remember that fifteen to thirty dollars invested in books on the subject is much better than three hundred dollars lost by not being sure what you have.

No matter what kind of a katana you buy, take care of it. It is one of a kind, and most important, it is yours. If you can learn Iaido with it, it will become you, with both your shortcomings and imagination. You would not let someone

Fig. 4A

open your head and touch your brain, so do not let anyone pull your sword from its *saya* and touch the skin. The swords of Japan have been said to be "the living souls of the Samurai." They were "the pride of Warriors and the theme of Pacts"[4]

The Samurai had just two things that were his and his alone. No man could take them from him. First was his honor and next it was his swords. His sword was regarded as the truest emblem of his virtue, valor, and strength. Mottos such as:

> There is nothing between heaven and earth that man need fear who carries at his side this magnificent blade.[5]

To exemplify this idea. The Samurai believed that:

> All weapons meant to kill are inconspicuous and never must be used except on occasions of extreme urgency. If any at all is to be used, however, let it be known that it is for the purpose of punishing evil and not for depriving one of life.[6]

I feel that it is very important to note at this time *(see Figures 4 & 4A)* the five elements of the universe; earth, metal, fire, water, and wood. All take their part in making the Japanese sword.

Formally Examining the Katana

The strictest of rules were observed by the Samurai in ancient times for examining the katana. Remember if you are a beginner in handling the sword, be extremely careful. First, because of the sharpness, and second, because if you drop the blade, you might damage or destroy its value as an object of great art.

First, you should purchase a cleaning kit which consists of oil, cleaning powder, and a brass tapper. Find a quiet place where you will not be disturbed. Take your katana out of its bag. Start by showing it the respect due an unknown person being introduced to you for the first time. You would shake hands in this country. But in Japan they would bow, so you should now bow to the blade. *(See Figures 5 & 5A.)*

Now holding the sword with your left hand, ha up, about half way down the saya, look at the *kodogu*, or "furniture." The furniture consists of all the metal ornaments and fittings on the sword except the blade itself. It is interesting to note that sometimes the kodogu are more valuable than the katana. Some pieces are made of gold and silver. Even the tsuba at times are signed and may be very valuable. Still holding the katana with your left hand and with the cutting edge up, start to pull the blade from the saya. *(See Figure 6.)*

---

[4] B.W. Robinson, *The Arts of the Japanese Sword*. Rutland, VT: C. E. Tuttle, Co., 1971. p. 15

[5] Donn F. Draeger, *Asian Fighting Arts*. New York, NY: Berkley Publishing Corp., 1969. p. 101

[6] D. T. Suzuki, *Zen and Japanese Culture*. Princeton, NJ: Princeton University Press, 1971.

Fig. 5

Fig. 5A

This should be done slowly. It is important to pull the saya from the katana and not the katana from the saya. Pull the blade out until you reach the kissaki. When you reach the kissaki, stop and examine it carefully. It is the most important part of the blade. When you have taken the sword all the way out of the saya, you may proceed to examine the blade. Laying down the saya, you may hold the sword in either hand. *(See Figure 7.)* Remember that it is not proper to examine the blade while you are taking it from the saya.

Fig. 6

Fig. 7

The best way to examine the blade now that it is out of the saya is to take a piece of soft clean cloth in one hand and rest the *shinogi* on it. *(See Figure 8.)* While you are examining the blade, be sure not to turn the ha or cutting edge toward anyone but yourself: this is most important.

After examining the blade for new rust marks, take the small brass tapper and remove the pin from the tsuba or handle. Taking the tsuba toward the bottom, in your right hand let the blade slant 35° Next, with the cutting edge up, hit your own right wrist with your left fist until the blade pops up. *(See Figure 9.)*

Fig. 8

Fig. 9

When the blade is loose from the handle, put the blade back in the saya. Now that the blade is safely put away, remove the tsuba from the tang or *nakago*. At this time you should remove all the hardware from the tang. Sometimes the habaki is very hard to remove, but if you work with it by using the brass tapper, it will come off easily. After examining the nakago, remove the blade again from the saya, using your right hand and the soft cloth in your left. The blade is now ready for cleaning. *(See Figure 10.)* Note that cleaning can be done with or without the handle in place.

Fig. 10

Cleaning the Katana

The first thing in cleaning the blade is to remove any oil that is now on it. After doing this, take the small round red ball that is in your cleaning kit (it has powdered limestone in it, called *uchiko*) and powder the entire blade. *(See Figure 11.)*

    After you have powdered the blade, take your cloth and give the blade forty to forty-five strokes on each side, always going up the blade from the back side so as not to cut yourself. The Samurai cleaned their swords everyday with forty to forty-five strokes. Always be very careful with the cleaning action; remember that if you get careless, the sword has a mind of its own and will remind you very painfully of your mistakes. After you have finished, wipe the blade clean with your cloth and go over the blade with the oil provided in your kit. There are several oils which you may use, such as mineral or vegetable, but the Japanese sword oil is the best, being made from cloves. After the blade has been serviced, replace all hardware and the handle, being careful not to touch the skin of the blade. After you have replaced the sword in the saya, cutting edge up, so that you do not drag the edge on the saya, replace it in your sword bag. This formal cleaning is only necessary about three or four times each year. But remember,

Fig. 11

when learning Iaido, you must clean the blade each and every time your lesson is finished. The cleaning after lessons consists only of wiping the blade down with a clean cloth; you need not use the powdered limestone. The powdered limestone has a cutting action like sandpaper and if used excessively, it will eventually take the yakiba off. After you have wiped the blade, put a thin coat of oil on it and return the blade to the saya. Take your time, get to know your Katana; it is probably a lot older than you.

One of the last things I would like to mention is how to show someone your sword. *(See Figure 12.)* If someone asks to see your katana and you wish them to look at it, always take the bottom part of the handle in your right hand, leaving plenty of room for the other person's hand. Place the cutting edge toward yourself and make sure that they have a firm grip on the handle before letting go.

Fig. 12

Kayano Wasuke Tsunenari (ronin of Ako)

CHAPTER TWO

Uniform Procedure

Hakama

The Iaido-gi consists of two pieces: the top jacket which can be white or dark blue and the *hakama* (pleated trousers). The white and black stitched top is usually worn by beginners. The hakama most commonly worn in practice is dark blue or black. Never mix your top and bottoms, like white top with a black bottom or black top with a white bottom. Of course, if you are a beginner, then the white top with the black stitching and the dark hakama is quite proper.

The hakama allows complete movement and its big bell-bottoms permit good air circulation when you are practicing Iaido.

Figure 13 shows you how to fold your top after practice. Never crumple-up your uniform after practice, remember the uniform is yours. Treat it with respect.

Fig. 13

Fig. 14   Fig. 15   Fig. 16

Fig. 17   Fig. 18   Fig. 19

Fig. 20	*Fig. 21*	*Fig. 22*

Putting on the hakama *(See Figure 14)*. As you step into the hakama, put the *koshi-ita* or stiffener to the back.

Now, pull the front up, take hold of the cords, wrap them behind you, and, changing hands, bring the cords to the front again. *(See Figure 15.)*

Now, crossing the cords in front about 3 inches down from the top waist band. *(See Figure 16.)*

Pull the cords to the rear and tie them in a bow. Make sure that your top is pulled down tight so that there is not a bulge in the back. *(See Figure 17.)*

Now pick up the back of the hakama with both hands. Place the koshi-ita over the bow and bring the cords to the front. *(See Figure 18.)*

Figures 16 & 19 show that all cords, front and back, are in line crossing to the front. Tie a small knot in the center where the cords cross.

After this, take one end and fold it back and forth across the knot *(See Figure 20)*, making all ends even.

When this is finished, take the other end and circle around the bow until there is nothing left. *(See Figure 21.)*

When you finish, it should look like *Figure 22*, with no ends showing.

Sageo

Sageo is the Japanese word used for the cord on the saya or scabbard. It has many uses, but the most important one to the Samurai or Bushi was for tying the sleeves of his kimono up out of the way to prepare for action.

Fig. 23

Fig. 24

Fig. 25

Fig. 26

I should point out that there are as many ryu (or schools) for the sageo as there are for Iaido. It would be safe to say each style of Iaido usually has its own Sageo method. Here we are dealing with the Mu-Gai-Ryu method.

Figure 23 illustrates making your formal bow and sitting in place *(seiza)*.

With the katana on your left side, the cutting edge away from you and the tsuba even with your left knee, take the sageo out of the kurigata. Note that this action may also be done after the katana is in the *obi* (or belt). Then, taking the sageo in your left hand, place one end in your mouth. *(See Figure 24.)*

Now, extending the right hand about three-fourths of the way out, use the left hand and place the sageo behind the right arm and behind the neck. Pull the sleeve up snug. *(See Figure 25.)*

Now using the right hand, take the sageo behind the left shoulder, catching the left sleeve, and bring it in front of the left arm and behind the neck, taking hold of the sageo with the right hand. *(See Figure 26.)*

Figure 27 shows a bow tied in the sageo over the right shoulder.

Figure 28 shows that the bow has been removed from sight by pulling on the sageo with the right hand using the sageo under the left arm.

Remember that the beginning of practice is as important as the end. The tying of the sageo by a sixteenth-century Samurai preparing for battle was indeed a sight to behold. The tying of the sageo could be done in about three seconds and with one hand. If the opposing Samurai could see that his opponent had mastered the sageo with the speed of lightning, but yet projected the stillness of a forest just before a storm, he might think twice before doing battle.

Fig. 27

Fig. 28

Chikamatsu Kanroku Yukishige (ronin of Ako)

CHAPTER THREE

Proper Sword Procedure

Iaido Dojo

You should always be aware of the tradition of the performance of Iai before a Shinto altar or before friends. Most importantly, never make a circus out of Iai. People will respect you and the art more—even if they themselves do not understand it—if you maintain the etiquette that the art deserves.

TEITO SHISEI:
Teito shisei is the formal standing position before you enter the dojo or place in which you are about to practice. *(See Figure 29.)* The katana or long sword is in the left hand with the cutting edge turned up. Your thumb should always be

Fig. 29

on the tsuba or sword guard at all times when you are moving the katana from one place to another or when you are carrying the sword. With the katana in the left hand, turn the end of the handle to the right one-half way between your navel and your right side with the end of the saya or scabbard pointing down about thirty to thirty-five degrees. The thumb on the left hand should slightly touch the waist or upper hip bone, depending on one's build. The left elbow is bent about twenty degrees and is relaxed. (Note that you should always remain relaxed—in every move).

Carrying the Katana

Always remember that the katana is a very dangerous weapon and that the Japanese have a great respect for it, as you will also if you know what you are doing when you carry one.

Note that you should never take the katana out of the saya or scabbard in jest or act as if you are about to draw it against someone. You would not take a real gun out and point it at another, unless you intended to do him harm: the Japanese feel the same way about the sword.

If you are in the dojo, the foot closest to the shrine or flag is the "upper foot." Go to the place in which you are going to practice with the shrine or flag on your left side. This is your front during the exercise. To change your direction, turn in the direction of your "upper foot." This "upper foot" is called *kami-no-ashi*.

The Formal Bow or Kamiza

Holding the katana in your left hand, handle to the front, blade slanting down about thirty-five degrees, stand erect, facing the shrine or flag. *(See Figure 29.)* Now reach across your body and take the katana below the saya or sword guard. *(See Figure 30.)*

Next, bring the katana to the right side of the body with the handle to the rear with the cutting edge pointing down and the kojiri pointing down thirty-five degrees. You must remember to stay completely relaxed. *(See Figure 31.)*

Now bow from the waist toward the shrine, flag, or dojo. Try to keep your head in line with your back. *(See Figure 32.)*

After the bow, take your left hand and grasp the saya below the tsuba and replace the katana on the left side of the body. *(See Figure 33.)*

Place your thumb on the tsuba. During outdoor practice, you may hold the katana horizontally above your head and bow.

Fig. 30

Fig. 31

Fig. 32

Fig. 33

Sitting in Place: Seiza

Holding the katana in your left hand, thumb on the tsuba, bend your knees about forty degrees. Then, reach down with your right hand and spread the hakama or skirt. This can be done quietly by pushing the loose material left to right behind the knees. Now kneel in place, first with the left knee and then the right. Try and keep your back as straight as possible. You should fix your eyes at a point about 3 feet in front of you on the floor. *(See Figure 34.)*

As you sit, bring both big toes together; and your feet should make a "v." *(See Figure 35.)*

Fig. 34

Fig. 35

The knees should be about 6–7 inches apart. Place your right hand on your right thigh and the katana on the left thigh. *(See Figure 36.)*

Now lay the katana to the left side of your left thigh, with the sword guard in line with your knee. The cutting edge must be turned toward your own body, about 6 inches away from your thigh. *(See Figure 37.)*

Fig. 36

Fig. 37

This is one of the most important parts of Iaido. You must sit erect, straightening the neck and the chest. Close your eyes and place both hands on your thighs. You must be completely relaxed at this point:

> Try to clear your mind of all things. This is called *mushin*. Remember; "The moon has no intent to cast its shadow anywhere, nor does the pond design to lodge the moon."[1]

After one or two minutes, open your eyes half way and focus them about 6 feet in front of you on the floor, forming a triangle with the fingers and touching the thumbs. *(See Figure 38.)*

Your upper body should be leaning forward about forty-five degrees. As you formally bow, both elbows touch the knees and the floor. Hold the bow for about a slow five count, then rise slowly and quietly return the right hand and then the left hand to the thighs. At this time you will again be in seiza.

Now take the left hand and grasp the saya just below the tsuba with your thumb on the tsuba and bring the katana to the left thigh. *(See Figure 39.)*

Fig. 38

Fig. 39

---

[1] Ibid. p. 116

Rise on the back of your feet by going straight up; push up with your thighs but do not lean forward. With your toes under the balls of your feet, you will be in a half-sitting position. Place the right foot against the inside of the left knee and stand erect. *(See Figure 40.)*

Be sure not to bend the waist while standing up. Align the left foot with the right foot.

Fig. 40

Sitting with Raised Knee: Iai-Hiza

If you are standing with the katana in your obi or belt, this is formally called *taito shisei*. From taito shisei you can go into iai-hiza. First, place your left thumb on the tsuba, keeping the left forearm next to your hip. Next, start to kneel, taking your right hand and placing the loose part of your hakama in back of your left knee. Now touch the left knee to the floor, placing your left foot on the floor so that you can sit on it with your right knee still raised. *(See Figures 41 & 42.)*

Now sit down: the left heel should be in the center of your body with the instep flat on the floor. You must keep your back and neck straight with the right hand on the right thigh and remain relaxed. While sitting on your left heel, let your right knee slant outwards about forty-five degrees. Pull the right heel in towards your left knee. Now place both hands on your upper thighs.

Fig. 41

Fig. 42

Preparation for Iaido Practice

You must remember that the Samurai of old Japan believed the highest level of Iai was *saya-no-unchi*, or invincibility without drawing the sword. So you might say greater than techniques is spiritual training. I believe Iai is a spiritual thing. You must learn to cut the enemy within yourself. If you can accomplish this, you will truly be on your way in Iai. This reminds me of a story of Saya-no-unchi:

One of Japan's greatest swordsman was Tsukahara Bokuden (1490–1572), who had great mastery of Saya-no-unchi. Bokuden was crossing Beira in a rowboat with a number of passengers. There was braggart among them; a rough-looking Samurai, stalwart and arrogant in every possible way. He boasted of his skill in swordsmanship, saying that he was the foremost man in the art. The fellow passengers were eagerly listening to his blatant talk, while Bokuden was dozing as if nothing were going on about him. This irritated the braggart very much. He approached Bokuden and shook him saying, "You also carry a pair of swords, why not say a word?" Bokuden answered quietly, "My art is different from yours; it consists not of defeating others, but in not being defeated." This incensed the fellow immensely. "What is your school then?" Bokuden replied, "Mine is known as the *mutekatsu* school" (which means to defeat the enemy without hands, that is, without using a sword). "Why, then, do you yourself carry a sword?" asked the Samurai. "This is meant to do away with selfish motives and not to kill others," answered Bokuden. The man's anger knew no bounds, and he exclaimed in a most impassioned manner, "Do you really mean to fight me with no swords?" "Why not?" was Bokuden's answer. The braggart Samurai called out to the boatman to row toward the nearest land. But Bokuden suggested that it would be better to go to the island farther off because the mainland might attract people who might somehow get hurt.

The Samurai agreed. The boat headed toward the solitary island at some distance. As soon as they were near enough, the man jumped off the boat and, drawing his sword, was all ready for combat. Bokuden leisurely took off his own swords and handed them to the boatman. To all appearance he was about to follow the Samurai onto the island, when Bokuden suddenly took the oar away from the boatman and pushing it against the land, gave a hard backstroke to the boat. There upon, the boat made a precipitous departure from the island and plunged into the deeper water safely away from the man. Bokuden smilingly remarked "This is my 'No Sword School.'"[1]

Through this story of Bokuden, I feel you can learn to defeat the enemy through his psychological weakness. The worst enemy each of us has is the one only we know about, the one inside of us. This is truly the Samurai's way of Iai.

---

[1] Ibid. pp. 74–75

In preparing to practice Iaido, you must first bow to the sword. After you are in the dojo and have bowed formally to the shrine or to the flag, take your practice position. *(See Figure 43.)*

You must sit with the shrine or flag on your left. While the left hand holds the katana, place the right hand on your left thigh. The ha is pointing up. With the left thumb on the tsuba, bring the katana forward and across the body. Reaching with the right hand, take hold of the saya just below the tsuba on the koikuchi with both thumbs on the tsuba. Now hold the sword guard between the right index and middle fingers. Pulling the katana to the right across the body, let the saya slide through your left hand between your hip and your thigh. *(See Figure 44.)*

Fig. 43

Fig. 44

Stop the saya in the left hand about 5 inches from the kojiri or end of the saya.

Now, with both hands, place the katana on the floor in front of you with the cutting edge away from you. Note to be sure to bring the end of the saya slightly to you and away from the shrine or flag. *(See Figure 45.)*

Position your hands as in *Figure 46*, bow.

Again, count to five slowly. Do not pop up after the bow but come up slowly. It might be good to note at this time that if you are in a formal class with a sensei or teacher, you should always raise your head only after he has his up. This is very important. Your head should always be a little lower than the sensei's when bowing.

You must now sit in the seiza position and close your eyes trying to reach spiritual preparation with your sword, readying yourself for action. This is called *zanshin* and is very important to a true student of Iaido. You must try to become one with your sword, thinking of it as a part of your body and not a weapon in your hand. Only when you can achieve this frame of mind will you be able to do Iaido smoothly and find that the significance of Iai is peace and harmony with the universe.

Fig. 45

Fig. 46

Having completed zanshin, lean forward, trying to keep your back and head as straight as possible. Place your right hand just below the tsuba on the koikuchi with the thumb holding the tsuba. Your left hand will hold the end of the saya about 4 inches from the end. *(See Figure 45.)* Lifting the katana to the right and holding the tsuba with your index finger, insert the katana in your obi or inner-sash. *(See Figures 46 & 46A.)*

The katana is now secured. Note, if your katana has a sageo and you are not using it to tie back your sleeves, it is proper at this time to take the sageo in your right hand and bring it across the body to your right side, taking the ends and looping them through your obi or intersash. Make sure you do not pull the sageo tight; it must be very loose. Tie the ends to the obi. Again, I must point out there are many different ways to secure the sageo according to the ryu. Now return the saya. With the Katana secured, align the tsuba with your navel. *(See Figure 46B.)*

Fig. 46A

Fig. 46B

Dattao
Removing the Katana from the Obi

Remember that the end of practicing Iaido is as important as the beginning and each move must be done as flowingly as a bird about to land on a pond. Holding the saya just below the tsuba with the right hand and pressing the tsuba with your thumb, slide the sword out of the obi to your right front. *(See Figures 47 & 47A.)*

Fig. 47

Fig. 47A

Removing the katana, be sure to let the left hand slide along the saya and stay at the hip. The ha faces your body. Slowly lay the katana down in front of you. *(See Figures 48 & 49.)*

Fig. 48

Fig. 49

The ha is toward the left. Your left hand stays on your hip and back. The back and neck remain straight. At this time, replace both hands on your thighs. *(See Figure 50.)*

Make your bow to the katana, returning your hands to the thighs. (*See Figure 51.*) Resume seiza and prepare for taijo.

Fig. 50

Fig. 51

Taijo
Procedure for Leaving the Practice Area

Keeping the left hand on the left thigh, grasp the saya with the right hand just below the tsuba. (Keep the index finger on the tsuba). Now raise the katana to a vertical position. *(See Figure 52.)*

Fig. 52

The ha should be toward you and the katana should be in the center of your knees, about one foot forward. Now put your left hand around the saya and gently slide the hand down to the end of the saya. *(See Figure 53.)*

Fig. 53

Lift the katana and place it on your lap with the end of the saya pointing to the rear. *(See Figure 54.)*

Now, quietly move the right leg forward and assume the formal stance. After you have stood up, take three steps backward. Turning to the place of honor—the shrine, or the flag—put the katana in the right hand and bow. Then return the katana to the left hand and leave the practice area. Note that if you have a teacher present, it would be proper to go to him at this time and bow. Do not carry your katana with you. When you have mastered all these things, you will be ready to start your lessons in drawing the sword from the saya.

Fig. 54

Fuwa Kazuemon Masatane (ronin of Ako)

CHAPTER FOUR

Nukikata—Drawing of the Sword

Kata Number One
Ippon Me Mae

MIND LIKE WATER

A reflection in water is the symbol of
a clear, calm mind in harmony with
its surrounding—the highest level of
training in a martial art.

Before we actually draw the sword, let me put you in the right frame of mind. I
have previously said you should try to empty your mind of the day's thoughts.
Close your eyes, think of something pleasant, something that has happened or
that you wish would happen. Let your shoulders relax. It is most important to
be relaxed before and during practice. Remember that if you throw a rock into a
pond, it makes a splash for only a second and then every drop of water returns
to its previous stillness, as nothing had happened. This is most important. The
draw must appear out of nowhere, in effect, "Now you see it, now you don't." I
do not want you to think this is done by a trick or by speed; it is something very
hard to explain. The best way I know to explain the appearance of the katana
in Iai is to compare it with hunting. Have you ever been hunting or deep in a
forest sitting very quietly? Everything stops and you can hear a pin drop. The
noise of the forest starts up again, everything is as it was with you as quiet and
relaxed as possible. You can see nothing unusual, your eyes look all around and
out of nowhere a deer or small animal appears, as if it had just materialized from
thin air. Now this is Iai—The movement becomes so natural that the sword just
seems to materialize from your hand.

There is no jerking movement, nothing out of the ordinary to catch the eye—
except that the first time they looked the sword was not in your hand, and the
next second it was. The first reaction people seem to have to this is, "How did
you do that?" A question that is impossible to answer.

Fig. 55

Attain the seiza position by kneeling with the knees 8 or so inches apart, place the big toes flat on the floor, and sit on your heels with your hands on your thighs. *(See Figure 55.)*

This kata starts as you sense the enemy about to attack you. You will cut his right temple just above the ear and then deliver the finishing cut of a downward stroke. This kata, as with all katas, starts with a breathing exercise. Take three deep breaths, letting each one half way out and then the rest. Now repeat this action, only this time—on the last breath—inhale, and while drawing the blade, exhale. Now, put your left hand on the koikuchi with the thumb on the tsuba and bring the end of the saya across your body. The tsuba or handle should be within reach of your right hand. Note that you do not reach across your body with your right hand to take hold of the handle. The reason for this is quite simple, in that you will expose your right *kote* (or wrist) to your opponent for a downward cut. Next, take the tsuba in your right hand and push with your left thumb against the tsuba, so that the blade has slipped out of the saya about ½ inch. At this time, push up with your legs, using mostly your thigh muscles. This motion will bring your body straight up instead of leaning forward with your head down exposing your neck to your opponent. When you have attained about one half of your height, bring your toes under your feet so that the balls of your feet are on the floor. Now, turn the saya so that the cutting edge of the katana is away from your body. This is done by giving the saya a half twist with your left hand, using the wrist only. Keep your head straight and your eyes on the floor, about 4 or 5 feet in front of you. Next, pull the blade out of the saya except for 2 or 3 inches. *(See Figure 56.)*

Now, as you pull the remaining 3–4 inches of the blade out of the saya, bring your right foot out in front of you making a 90° angle with your thigh and the calf of your right leg. This is a horizontal cut. *(See Figure 57.)*

You should stamp the floor as the sword comes to a stop so that the body and the sword end the movement at the same time. Note that your left shoulder should be pulled back slightly and your rear foot should have only the ball on the floor. For a rear view of this *see Figure 57A.*

Fig. 56

Fig. 57

Another point to keep in mind while making this cut is that you should pull the end of the saya (koikuchi) away from your body so that the kojiri or tip of the saya is even with your right knee. *(See Figure 58.)*

Fig. 57A

Fig. 58

Again, do not be too anxious to do the next movement until you have studied the previous drawings carefully. *(Refer back to Figures 56 & 57.)* As you see in *Figure 58*, the correct movement in holding the kuchi is that the little finger should be on the obi and the elbow should be pulled to the rear. This movement is called *sayabiki* or saya pulling. *Figure 59* indicates that the wrist should not be bent and *Figure 60* indicates that the little finger is not touching the obi. It also shows that the wrist does not touch the waist, which would be incorrect.

Fig. 59

Fig. 60

If you have studied these last movements in depth, you are now ready to start the killing blow or the downward cut. *Figure 61* illustrates how to bring the katana around to the left side of the head, keeping the blade straight and the cutting edge away from you.

The wrist should not be bent. Next, take a step with your left knee, and by pushing with the ball of your left foot, align your left knee with the heel of your right foot. This action is done by keeping a low profile. Do not raise and lower your body. Now, raise the katana above your head quickly, but not in a jerking movement and take hold of the handle with the left hand. *(See Figure 62.)*

The hands and the sword should be in the direct center of your body and the blade should be vertical. Note that some ryu teach letting the back or shinogi of the blade touch the back to make this cut. If you do practice this cut that way, you will develop a stronger cut, but with a slower movement. I find it very helpful to practice these movements in a mirror so that incorrect technique can easily be seen.

Fig. 61

Fig. 62

Fig. 63

As you pull the blade forward, making a circle over your head, bring the right foot forward and stamp the foot at the same time you complete your cut. *(See Figure 63.)*

Keep your back and head straight. Do not lock your elbows. The body should have moved forward about 1½ feet, and the blade will be at a 45° angle. The tsukagashira of the handle will be pointing at your navel. To complete this cut, stop the katana with the tsukagashira of the handle still pointing at the navel and the end of the blade about one foot from the floor. The hand movements for this and all two-handed cuts will be like wringing out a wet towel; right and left hands twisting inward to the center of the handle. Your hands should be on the menukis of the handle. You have now completed the cutting action of this kata. *(See Figure 64.)*

Your next movement will be the *chiburi* or removing the blood from the blade. *(See Figure 65.)*

Fig. 64

Fig. 65

Place your left hand on the saya, and push the sword a little forward turning the cutting edge to your right and bringing the sword up to the right side of the body with the blade horizontal and with the elbow slightly bent. Now bring the katana up close to the top of your ear (this is done by just bending the elbow). *(See Figure 66.)*

While keeping your back and head straight, simultaneously rise to your feet and make a circle over your head. Stop the blade about 40° downward and even with your right knee. This action should be done with the knees spread slightly outward and sinking at the waist. The right and left hand should be on the same line and your eyes focused 5 or 6 feet in front of you. *(See Figure 67.)* Note that the movement of shaking the blood off of the katana is like snapping a whip and is mostly a wrist action technique.

Fig. 66

Fig. 67

Now, bring the left foot up even with the front right foot. Stay in a squatting position and do not allow your body to move up and down. *(See Figure 68.)*

Holding this squatting position with the knees bent just a little, bring the right foot to the rear. *(See Figure 69.)* Note that the rest of your body does not move from its previous position.

Fig. 68

Fig. 69

Figure 70 illustrates the starting movements for the blade's return to the saya: move the left hand and place it around the opening of the saya, turning the saya sideways in your obi using the middle finger and thumb. Place the back of the blade about where the mune is between your left index finger and thumb. Note that if you are using a real sword, you must be extremely careful at this point so that you do not cut your thumb on the return of the blade.

Now, slide the blade out to the very tip holding it still with only your forefinger and thumb. When you feel the end (*kissaki*) of the blade reach the opening of the saya (*koikuchi*), start to push back so that the blade will start on its way into the saya, you will have to release your grip on the handle just a little, holding the handle (*tsuka*) with your fingers and thumb. Remember to keep your back and head straight, looking ahead and keeping your knees bent. *(See Figure 71.)*

Fig. 70

It should be mentioned here that it would be best to look down at the saya a few times until you get the feel for this movement. Always remember a true Iai practitioner never looks down on the return because the sword and you are one. You do not look down when you put your hand in your pocket, do you?

Simultaneously slide the saya to the tsuba and the blade in the saya. Turn the saya up so that the cutting edge is pointing upwards. All this is done while you are lowering your right knee to the floor. Keeping your back and neck straight, tilt your head just a little and focus your eyes on a spot ahead of you. When the tsuka has reached the koikuchi, slide the katana back in your obi or belt just a little by placing your left thumb on the tsuba. *(See Figure 72.)*

When you have completed this movement, rise to your feet, pushing up with the ball of your rear foot. When you stand up do not lean forward, but go straight upward. Now, align your front foot with your back foot by stepping back with your left foot. Replace your right hand to your side and assume taito shisei position. *(See Figure 73.)*

This completes the first Kata: lppon Me Mae. This kata should be practiced at least five hundred times before proceeding to the next kata. Keep in mind all the small movements it requires as you would keep in mind all the ingredients necessary to make a good stew.

Fig. 71

Fig. 72

Fig. 73

Isogai Jurozaemon Masahisa (ronin of Ako)

Kata Number Two
Nihon Me Ushiro
(Behind Rear Drawing)

Nihon Me Ushiro, or attacking from behind to the front, begins with the seiza position. *(See Figure 64.)*

Remember that the kata starts with your hands on your thighs and the tsuba of the katana even with your navel or the center of your body. Note that as you start this kata, your back is to the flag or the shrine. Your big toes are touching and the tops of your feet are flat on the floor. *(See Figure 74A.)*

The movement of this kata occurs when the enemy is behind you; you will make a 180° turn to the rear and cut his right temple.

As you begin to raise your body using your thigh muscles, turn the katana sideways with the cutting edge away from you and slowly start the blade out of the saya. Now bring the toes under the ball of the right foot and start the left leg up, turning 180° to the left by pivoting on the right knee. *(See Figure 75.)*

You are now facing the front of the enemy. Stamp the left foot on the floor as you complete this horizontal cut, cutting the enemy on the right temple. *(See Figure 76.)*

Now complete the other thirteen movements as in kata number one. Everything remains the same except that the foot movement is reversed. Remember:

> Our brains are given to us as instruments capable of a specific, a limited task. When trying to understand the real mysteries, the brain stops short. The brain can contain neither the questions themselves, nor the answers. To come to real understanding, to enlightenment, quite another instrument has to be used, intuitive insight.[1]

---

[1] Van de Wetering, J., *The Empty Mirror*. Boston: The Houghton Mifflin Co., pp. 8–9

Fig. 74

Fig. 74A

Fig. 75

Fig. 76

Horibe Yahyoe Kanemaru (ronin of Ako)

Kata Number Three
Ukenagashi
(Warding off Drawing)

By the time a student encounters the third kata, he should be discovering that Iaido is an art, and like many other arts in Japan it is seen as a way of enlightenment. The technical training of stances, cuts, blocks, etc. must be combined with the spiritual training of the "way" if the ultimate goal of Iaido is to be reached: the sword of no sword. From the viewpoint of purely technical skill, the beginner and master are the same. All knowledge is a circle, for both the master and the beginner move instinctively, without any cognition between perception and correct response. Once the first technique is learned then the student is no longer a beginner and he is on the way. He must either continue to travel the circular path that is the way, or discover that he would have been better off never having learned his first technique.

In this kata, Ukenagashi, the enemy is to your left and he suddenly attacks you. Starting from seiza, remove your hands from your thighs and place them on your katana as in kata number two. Do not forget to push the tsuba with your thumb. Rise straight up, using your thigh muscles, but tilting your body just a little forward about twenty degrees and to the right. Turning the upper part of your body and head to face the attacker, start your draw. The cutting edge of your blade is upward. *(See Figure 77.)*

Fig. 77

Draw the blade out close to your chest and then raise it over the head ,slanting the tip downward about 35 degrees to ward off the opponent's attack. This movement is done with the left foot forward. *(See Figure 78.)*

Fig. 78

Now, standing up, right foot to the rear, keeping the knees bent, bring the right foot to the heel of the left foot. The left heel should be turned outward. *(See Figure 79.)*

You have blocked the enemy's sword. Step to the rear with the left foot turning about 90 degrees to your left, facing your enemy. This turning movement is done when you have taken hold of the handle of your sword with both hands and delivered a downward stroke to the enemy's left shoulder. The downward stroke stops with the tsuka at the middle of your waist and the tip about even with the middle of your stomach. The cutting edge of the blade should be angled to the left just a little. *(See Figure 80.)*

Fig. 79

While holding this position, bend your front knee a little, which in this case is your right knee. Bring the handle up and to the left side of your body and slightly release the grip with your right hand. Then place the end of the blade about 6 inches up from the knee on your right leg. *(See Figure 81.)*

The right hand should be next to the tsuba with the hand open, but holding the handle between the thumb and index finger.

At this time regrip the handle as in *Figure 82*, turning the right hand over.

Hold the handle firmly with your left hand, but only with the fingers and thumb of your right. You must be ready at any time for the enemy's possible counterattack.

Fig. 80

Fig. 81

Fig. 82

Next, while still keeping your eyes on the opponent, remove your left hand from the handle and take hold of the opening of the saya making ready for the return. *(See Figure 83.)*

Holding the handle of the sword with your fingers and thumb of your right hand, bring the back of the blade to the left hand. Note that you should place the back of the blade between the thumb and the index finger of the left hand about midway down from the tsuba. *(See Figure 84.)*

Fig. 83

Fig. 84

The tip of the blade will be pointing to the rear with the cutting edge away from your body. Start pulling the back of the blade between your left index finger and thumb. Bring the handle out and to the left of your body. When you feel the kissaki or tip of the blade between your thumb and finger, place it in the koikuchi of the saya. Start the return. Note that the blade is still turned with the cutting edge away from you. This movement is executed while you are bending the left knee. When your left knee is about halfway from the floor, turn the saya upward so that the cutting edge is now up and you are letting the blade ride on the mune. Continue down until the left knee touches the floor. The movement of the blade and the knee end at the same time. *(See Figure 85.)*

Using the ball of the left foot and the right thigh muscles rise to your feet. Bring the left foot to the right foot. Note that when rising you do not lean forward but come straight up, keeping your eyes on the opponent or on the floor 5–6 feet in front of you. After aligning your feet, take your right hand off of the handle and bring it to your side. Place your left thumb on the tsuba and assume the taito shisei. *(See Figure 86.)*

Fig. 85

Fig. 86

Chiba Saburobei Mitsutada (ronin of Ako)

CHAPTER FIVE

Seppuku (Abdomen Cutting)

In recent decades, Japan's legends and feudal practices have become familiar to many of us. By far the most talked about is seppuku. When you read something about one cutting himself open, somehow the mind always goes back to the Japanese and asks the question, "Why would anyone do such a thing?" First, I think you would have to be Japanese to understand. Many books and endless talking to some of the old Japanese masters have led me to understand the Japanese feeling about the subject. But I must confess I do not understand how men could do such a thing in the frame of mind in which they did it.

Many Westerners with whom I've discussed the subject seem to feel that the act of seppuku was committed in a drugged or drunken state. To be sure you understand seppuku or hara-kiri (abdomen cutting), let me make this clear; At no time were those men committing seppuku under the influence of any drugs or drink. On the contrary, their minds were as clear as crystal and knew what they were doing every minute. Seppuku, the formal name, and hara-kiri, the more common word for the practice, go back in Japanese history to about 1336 CE. Before this time, it was the custom in crimes deserving capital punishment to either behead or to strangle the condemned person—not much different than the European custom of hanging or the French custom of using the guillotine. (And I might add, preferable to being burned at the stake or being stoned to death by a mob.) I am not suggesting that seppuku was a pleasant way to die, but for the Japanese it was a way for them to die with honor and self-respect, and to keep their name clean.

Today most of us feel that there is no particularly "good" way of putting an end to one's life, but if you were born a warrior, or Samurai, in Japan, the way you died was very important to you and your family. I think elements of the same sentiment are evident even in our society today. If a member of your family committed a capital crime and was executed, you would be reluctant to discuss the death socially. On the other hand, if the relative committed suicide in a very brave and dramatic way before being arrested for his offense, his death tends to elicit social compassion and sympathy rather than the disdain shown a convicted murderer.

During the period of time in Japan's history that seppuku was customary, only Samurai were allowed to practice this manner of suicide. The act of seppuku had as many formalities as would a White House state dinner for visiting nobility.

The Samurai was well trained in the ceremony of seppuku because he might have to take a role in it or at least might have to teach it to younger Samurai just beginning their journey as warriors. First, it was necessary to select witnesses, then find a place for the condemned man to wait. Next, a location for the ceremony had to be determined and then "seconds" had to be selected. A second was one of the most important men in the ceremony; he had to be chosen very carefully and was usually agreed to by the condemned man. A Samurai who acted as a second was called *kaishaku*. The kaishaku was required to be of sound mind and body. He was to show neither his like nor dislike for the office given him. The kaishaku wore a formal dress called a *hempen*, with the hakama tucked under the belt. In the ceremony, he must not wear his sword, but should have a small knife hidden upon him somewhere. There were three seconds in the ceremony, the head kaishaku, his assistant and a lower class kaishaku. It is the duty of the head second to cut off the condemned man's head and this is the most important position in the ceremony of seppuku. The assistant kaishaku handles the tray upon which the small knife with which the condemned man cuts himself open is placed. The third kaishaku carries the severed head to the witnesses for identification. The third man is also important because he might be called upon to cut off the head if something should happen to the other two men.

It is very interesting to note that the second who cuts off the head is not allowed to use his own sword, but must use the condemned man's own weapon. The reason for this being if a mishap in the beheading occurs, it can be blamed on the victim's sword and not the kaishaku. It is the second's job to decapitate the condemned man with a single blow. You might think this a simple thing to do, especially for a Samurai trained to use the sword almost from the time he could walk, but let me add one further point: the head had to be cut off, except for a little piece of skin which was to keep the head from falling off the platform and touching the ground. To cut off a man's head this way, the Samurai had to know precisely what he was doing and have extraordinary control. He and his sword had to be as one.

When all was prepared for the ceremony of seppuku and the condemned man had bathed, fixed his hair, put on his white formal clothes, and said his good-byes to his close friends, he was lead out to the mats where the ceremony was to take place. *(See Figure 87.)*

Fig. 87

At this time, according to his rank, he might ask for a pen and paper to write his farewells. This was kept to an acceptable minimum of time. The second should be to the left and out of sight of the condemned man. The condemned man faced west and the second faced the north. When the condemned man had put his writing implements down, the second made himself ready. The condemned man at this time stripped himself from the waist up, tucking his upper clothing under his knees and legs tightly so as to support his body. This was done so his body would fall forward and not backward. At this time the condemned man reached out and grasped the dirk or small knife. Pointing the dirk to himself and inserting it into his stomach with both hands, he drew it across his stomach from left to right, twisting the knife and pulling it up to the solar plexus, by following the lower rib. This done, he withdraw the dirk and laid it down. Not a sound is to be heard from the condemned man or anyone else at the ceremony. *(See Figure 88.)*

The second then stepped to the left and placed himself in position to strike the final blow. The condemned man leaned forward and extended his neck. The kaishaku who has followed every movement of the condemned man, now without delay, raises his katana and with the speed of lightning removes the head from the body (all but a tiny piece of skin under the chin). If this is accomplished, the kaishaku has done his job well. *(See Figure 89.)*

Fig. 88

Note: Laying down thick paper and placing the head on it shows a disposition to pay respect to the head; to place it on the edge of the sword is insulting: the course pursued must depend upon the rank of the person. If the ceremony is to be curtailed, it may end with the cutting off of the head; that must be settled beforehand, in a consultation with the witnesses. In the event of the second making a false cut, so as not to strike off the head at a blow, he must take the head by the top knot, press it down, and cut it off. Should he take poor aim and cut into the shoulder by mistake and should the principal rise and cry out, before he has time to writhe, he should hold him down and stab him to death, and then cut off his head, or the assistant seconds, who are sitting behind, should come forward and hold him down, while the chief second cuts off the head. It may be necessary for the second, after he has cut off the head, to push down the body, and then pick up the head for inspection. If the body does not fall at once, which is said to be sometimes the case, the second should pull the feet to make it fall.[1]

Fig. 89

---

[1] A. B. Mitford (Lord Redesdale), "Appendix A: An Account of the Hara-Kiri," *Tales of Old Japan*. Rutland, VT: Charles E. Tuttle Co., 1970.

Ohishi Chikara Yoshikane (ronin of Ako)

CHAPTER SIX

Iai-Hiza Division

Kata Number Four
Tsuka-Ate
(Tsuka Striking)

This kata starts with you sitting in the iai-hiza position. (See page 49.) When you are threatened from the front and rear, Tsuka-ate could be applied. This consists of striking the front attacker in the solar plexus with the end of the handle, thrusting at the rear attacker with the blade and then finishing off the front attacker with a downward cut.

With this kata you are confronted with two attackers, and the most important thing to remember is not to let your mind dwell on any one object or on the movement of the attackers.

> For instance, suppose ten men are opposing you, each in succession ready to attack you with a sword. As soon as one is disposed of, you will move on to another without permitting the mind to stop with any action. However rapidly one blow may follow another you leave no time to intervene between the two. Every one of the ten will thus be successively and successfully dealt with. This is possible only when the mind moves from one object to another without being "stopped" or arrested by anything. If the mind is unable to move on in this fashion, it is sure to lose the game somewhere between two encounters.[1]

To expand on mind-stopping would take a book in itself and I am by no means a Zen master able to teach these things. As my master once told me, I can only show you the way, I cannot teach you; you must teach yourself. As I have told you before, you must become one with your sword. Before you attempt this kata though, I want you to think about what I have said: Do not be like so many other people who read the beginning, the middle, and the end of a book and then tell everyone how wonderful or how terrible it was.

To state it in terms of swordsmanship, the genuine beginner knows nothing about the way of holding and managing the sword, and much less of his concern for himself. When the opponent tries to strike him, he instinctively parries it. This is all he can do. But, as soon as the training starts, he is taught how to

---

[1] Ibid. p. 98

handle the sword, where to keep the mind, and many other technical tricks—which makes his mind "stop" at various junctures. For this reason whenever he tries to strike the opponent he feels unusually hampered—He has lost altogether the original sense of innocence and freedom. But as days and years go by, as his training acquires fuller maturity, his bodily attitude and his way of managing the sword advance toward "no-mind-ness" which resembles the state of mind he had at the very beginning of training when he knew nothing, when he was altogether ignorant of the art. The beginning and the end thus turn into next-door neighbors. First, we start counting one, two, three, and when finally ten is counted, we return to one.[2]

You must believe me when I tell you that there are no short cuts in Iaido. Each person entering into the art must labor in slow pain like a mother giving birth. Only after the birth of her child, can she explain the highs and lows of it.

Figure 90 illustrates sitting in iai-hiza.

Fig. 90

Fig. 90A

---
[2] Ibid. pp. 99–100

Fig. 90B

As you are facing the shrine, place both hands on the katana with the right hand on the handle and the left hand on the saya. Do not push the tsuba with your thumb. Pushing up with the side of the right foot and lifting upward with the thigh of the left leg, rise to your left knee. Stamp the right foot on the floor as you bring the katana and saya forward to strike the enemy in front of you with the end of the handle of your katana. Note that the end of the handle, the tsukagashira, will be extended at arm's-length and even with your own solar plexus. *(See Figure 91.)*

Fig. 91

Now, pull the saya back with your left hand to your obi, and continue pulling the katana out of the saya with your left hand. Your body should be centered with your left knee and the top of your body leaning to the left at 40–45°. *(See Figure 92.)* You now see the enemy behind you, and the katana has cleared the saya. Turn the handle so that the cutting edge of the blade is away from you and so that the katana is horizontal with the floor. It should also be halfway between your solar plexus and your waist, close to your chest. *(See Figure 93.)*

Fig. 92

Fig. 93

Now, without changing your position, extend the right elbow and thrust to the enemy's solar plexus. Keep your back and head straight. Do not allow yourself to slump in this movement. *(See Figure 94.)*

Pulling the katana over your head, take hold of the handle with the left hand. Turn your body back to the front and deliver a downward cut to your first opponent. *(See Figure 95.)* While remaining in this position, execute chiburi (or shaking off the blood). This is done on the right side. Be sure to keep your left palm on your hip.

Fig. 94

Fig. 95

While you are holding the downward cut, let go of the handle with your left hand, replacing it on your waist and with your right hand bring the blade to your right side with the cutting edge away from you. The blade should be even with your right knee, but at arm's-length, with the wrist bent upward slightly and the kissaki lowered. *(See Figure 96.)*

Move the katana slightly forward, turning the blade edge to the left. Next, raise the sword from the floor even with your shoulder, with the kissaki away from you. The elbow is slightly turned toward the inside. Now, bending your elbow so that the tsuba is about 1½ inches from your temple, arc the blade over your head and stop in the same position in which you started the movement. *(See Figure 96 again.)*

To return the katana to the saya, place your left hand around the koikuchi of the saya and bring the hand to your navel. Place the back of the blade between your thumb and index finger about 3 inches from the kissaki. Now, pull the blade outward until you feel the tip in your thumb and finger. Remember to keep your back straight and your eyes on the floor in front of you. Now, start the return. *(See Figure 97.)*

Fig. 96

Fig. 97

As you are returning the blade to the saya, slide the right foot to the rear and align it with your left. Do not raise the body in this movement. With the feet aligned, you will be sitting on the heel of your left foot with the ball of the foot on the floor. The left knee will slowly decline to the floor and the right knee will be 90° to the right. Your thighs will be forming an "L" shape. The ball of the right foot will be on the floor. *(See Figure 98.)*

Now, with your left thumb on the tsuba, bring your right knee to the front. Next, with the tsuba in the center of your body, rise to the standing position (taito shisei). Align the rear foot with the front and remove the right hand from the handle.

This is the last of the sitting katas in this ryu. But always remember that the last of one thing is the beginning of another. Be sure you know where you have been so that you can return, before you start out for places unknown.

> When the sword is in the hands of a technician swordsman skilled in its use, it is no more than an instrument with no mind of its own. What it does is done mechanically, and there is no myoyu discernible in it. But, when the sword is held by the swordsman whose spiritual attainment is such that he holds it as though not holding it, it is identified with the man himself, it acquires a soul, it moves with all the subtleties which have been imbedded in him as a swordsman. The man emptied of all thoughts, all emotions originating from fear, all sense of insecurity, all desire to win, is not conscious of using the sword; both man and sword turn into instruments in the hands, as it were, of the unconscious, and it is this unconscious that achieves wonders of creativity. It is here that swordplay becomes an art.[3]

Fig. 98

---

[3] Ibid. p. 146

Hazama Shinroku Mitsukaze (ronin)

CHAPTER SEVEN

Happo-no-Kamae

"It is absurd to generate a tornado with bare hands. It is also magic to throw a dagger from underneath sleeves." The swordsman, Genshin Shinmen, claims that if you can handle two swords (one in each hand) with perfect control, then you are able to beat your opponent who holds one sword. This is not absurd nor magic. He also says that, if you keep on learning the way of two swords, you will be as good as an imperial guard of Han.[*]

Iai dojo

---

[*] Han: A Chinese dynasty dated 207 BCE–220 CE and marked by centralized control through an appointive bureaucracy, a revival of learning, and the penetration of Buddhism. (The Merriam-Webster Dictionary)

As I have stated before, drawing the sword out of the saya is Iai, but once it has been taken out of its resting place, you have Kenjutsu or Kendo offensive swordsmanship. In this chapter, I would like to talk about Happo-no-Kamae and Happo-Giri. Happo-no-Kamae translated means "style of eight directions" and Happo-Giri means "cutting style of eight directions." In a self portrait of Miyamoto Musashi *(see Figure 99)*, he holds his swords in a ready position

Fig. 99

HAPPO-NO-KAMAE
(A style of 8 directions)

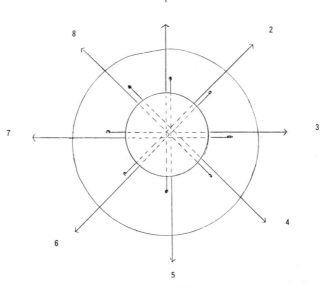

Fig. 100

known as "happo-biraki," or "open on all eight sides." It was believed that with this on-guard position there were no possible openings for attack. No book on swordsmanship would be complete without mentioning the greatest swordsman of his time, Master Miyamoto Musashi (Kensei), "Sword Saint" of Kenjutsu. Master Musashi was born in a Japanese village called Miyamoto in the province of Mimashaka in 1584 on the outskirts of Edo, or present-day Tokyo. He died in a cave, where he lived alone for the last two years of his life, in May of 1645, leaving his famous book "Five Rings" to his ken students. It is said that his book explaining the sword and life itself is still used by businessmen in Japan today. If only half the things that I have heard and read about him are true, he was a remarkable man indeed. It is said he had over sixty duels before he was twenty-nine years old and won all of them. Imagine discovering an old sword that was made in his era in someone's attic. Who knows, Musashi might even have used it, or fought against the person who did own it. There are no ends to the mysteries of Japanese swords.

I do not know if Musashi was an expert in Iai. In most of the accounts I have read, and in the stories my Kendo teachers in Japan have told me, he is portrayed with his swords out of the saya before the duel. Nevertheless, I know he had to be a master of the arts of Happo-no-Kamae and Happo-Giri. In *Figures 100, 101 & 101A–C*, you can see the circle of life with the eight points of directions.

Fig. 101

7 ←   → 3

Fig. 101A

Fig. 101B

Fig. 101C

These are the same eight points of off-balance every martial art uses today. Nothing really changes, does it? Life proceeds in a circle until we find the end, which only turns out to be the beginning of something new.

If you are standing in the center of this circle and holding your katana in chudan-no-kamae, or middle readiness, point the kissaki of the blade at your opponent's throat. If you have no opponent, point the kissaki at your own throat. The handle should be about even with your waist and one fist away from your body. For proper handle grip, see Chapter 12, "Sword Testing," page 153, *Figure 155*. The right hand should be forward. Now, not leaving the spot where you are standing, turn slowly 360 degrees, keeping an eye on the kissaki as you move and you will find your circle. This circle is the outer perimeter of your defense.

HAPPO-NO-KAMAE
(A style of 8 directions)

Fig. 102—Chudan-no-Kamae
(Middle)

Fig. 102A—Gedan-no-Kamae
(Down)

Each person's circle is different depending on his build and size. Needless to say, you have the same circle whether you are doing Kendo or Iaido. You may spend many hours wondering what I am talking about here, but your circle is the most important thing you will ever learn. You must not give up on it, the circle must become a part of you and your sword. Maybe I can explain it this way; You have

Fig. 102B—Hidari-Jodan-no-Kamae
(Up Left)

Fig. 102C—Migi-Jodan-no-Kamae
(Up Right)

Fig. 102D—Hidari-Hassou-no-Kamae
(Left up even with chin)

Fig. 102E—Migi-Hassou-no-Kamae
(Right up even with chin)

102F—Hidari Waki-no-Kamae
(Down Left)

102G—Migi-Waki-no-Kamae
(Down Right)

always had a circle with you; it is the extension of your hand at arm's-length. When you reach out, you never think anything about it, and if the object is just a little out of reach your mind tells you that you have to lean over to get it. This is where most accidents happen; you may lose your balance and sometimes fall. In Kenjutsu, that moment your mind was clouded with the thought of moving, you could be struck down. You must know your circle with your sword as if it were your hand.

Once your opponent has entered your circle with the tip of his sword, he can be cut down. If you look at *Figure 90* again, you will find the inner circle where the small line ends is where the cut should occur. In Iaido, facing to line 1, you can cut and block on any of these eight lines. As shown on pages 105–107, *Figures 102 & 102A–G*, you can see the different ready positions for on-guard readiness.

Pages 108–109, *Figures 103 & 103A–G*, demonstrate the eight different cutting styles of the eight directions. These should be studied until they are automatic to the mind.

Happo-Giri

(Cutting-style of 8 directions)
Happo-Giri
Hachi-No-Giri

Fig. 103—Morote-Tsuki
(Push to the front)

Fig. 103A—Hidari-Ichimonji-Giri
(Cut horizontally from left side)

Fig. 103B—Migi-Ichimonji-Giri
(Cut horizontally from right side)

Fig. 103C—Suichyoku-Giri
(Vertically from up to down)

Fig. 103D—Hidari-Kesa-Giri
(Cut down across from upper right side)

Fig. 103E—Migi-Kesa-Giri
(Cut down across from upper left side)

Fig. 103F—Hidari-Joho-Giri
(Cut up across from lower right side)

Fig. 103G—Migi-Joho-Giri
(Cut up across from lower left side)

Onodera Junai Hidekazu

CHAPTER EIGHT

Iaido Bujitsu

When working with the sword as I have said before, it must become one with you. It must become implanted, as if a working part of your body, in the unconscious mind. To point this out, let me refer to a story that I use in class. Have you ever been engrossed in something, it does not matter what, but deeply involved in your work? Suddenly and unexpectedly someone says something to you. You are startled and jump, raising your hand or hands up to your face for protection. Have you ever asked yourself why you reacted that way? It is your subconscious mind at work. Your subconscious has taken over the movement of your body without the body having any knowledge of it until the movement is finished. The subconscious part of your mind has used your body without letting the brain know about it until the danger has passed. This is how the sword must work in your hand with Iaido. Your motion must be so smooth that your mind, body and sword all move together. Only the subconscious mind really knows that the sword is not really a part of you.

There are three stages of mind control in swordsmanship. There is an ancient story about this. There once lived an old sword master in Kyushu who was about to retire from teaching Kenjutsu. He had three sons and before he retired, he had to select one as his successor. So he invited his best friend to his house to help with the selection. Upon the arrival of his friend, as was the custom in those days, he invited him to have a cup of tea. While they were drinking their tea and talking, they decided to play a small game with the three sons as a sort of test of their martial arts training as well as their physical ability. They placed a large heavy pillow above the door to their quarters so that when the door opened the pillow would fall and hit the person who entered. Upon completion of this task they made ready and the father called out to his youngest son to come to his aid. After about two or three minutes with no response, the father called out again, and in a loud voice the son answered, "Just a minute, Father." The father and his guest smiled at each other while sipping their tea. In a few minutes the son came to the door, opened it and stepped in. At the moment he entered the room down came the heavy pillow. But before it could land on his head, the young man jumped aside drawing his sword with lightning speed, cutting the pillow in half. Then after looking all around the room with sword in hand waiting for further action and feeling that the danger had passed, he replaced the sword in the saya and kicked the two halves of the pillow out of the way. He then bowed to the guest and then to his father, asking what his father wanted with him. The father introduced him to his best friend saying, "This is my youngest son. As you can see he is as fast as the hunting falcon." Dismissing the youngest son, he instructed him not to say a word about what had happened to his brothers. They then called for the next son. The next oldest son did not respond immediately, but it was not necessary to call him the second time. Arriving at the door, the son knocked and upon hearing his father reply, slid the door open and stepped in. Again, a heavy pillow came crashing down. The young man reached for his sword, but, instead of drawing, he caught the pillow in his hands. Turning his head to his father with a bewildered look, he replaced the pillow above the door. Bowing to his father's friend and then to his father, he asked what service he could be to them? The father introduced him saying, "This is my middle son, he has the eyes and calmness of a tiger before the kill." Instructing this son as the one before, they called for the eldest. Now the oldest son came at once and knocked on the door. The father called to him to enter, but the door did not move. After a second or two the father again bade him enter. This time the oldest son slid the door open about a foot, smiling through the doorway at his father and his father's friend. The son reached up through the doorway, took the pillow down, stepped through the doorway and replaced the pillow above the door. Turning to his father's guest, the son gave him a long and low bow, then turned to his father and also bowed. At this the father remarked to his friend. "This is my son, Kira, he is almost as wise as I. We think we are different only because we agree to think so." The friend bowed to the oldest son and said, "You have learned your lessons very well; you are surely your father in his youth. Your father has been the needle, and you the thread. Now you have become the needle." At this the friend bowed again, said his farewells, and departed.

When looking at the fourth kata, Ippon Me Mae, you can see in *Figures 104* through *107* the movement of the blade a little more clearly. The movement of the down stroke is a little different, going to the right side of the body instead of to the left. This is from the Mori-Ryu Iaido, but the results are the same. It is a good idea to practice both sides, because sometimes space will not allow a left-sided finishing cut.

Fig. 104

A woodblock print depicting Ichikawa Danzo III as a Samurai Drawing a Sword, ca. 1772. Courtesy of The Howard Mansfield Collection, Purchase, Rogers Fund, 1936.

Armor and armor carrier box.

Author Darrell Max Craig.

Students training in an Iaido dojo.

Calligraphy on the Te-nugui by the Buddhist Priest at the Hokkeji Shrine for the 13th Memorial Service for the late Harutane Chiba. The mountain in the center of the Te-nugui says, Ki, Ken, Tai – meaning, Spirit, Sword, and Body.

Harutane Chiba Sensei and the author demonstrating Chiba Hokoshin Ito Ryu, Kenjitsu kata.

Armor carrier box.

Author Darrell Max Craig.

Mt. Fuji test cut made by the author.

Imperial Palace Dojo, Tokyo, Japan. Setsuji Kobayashi Sensei and the author.

Harutane Chiba Sensei and the author at a Japanese festival.

Haga Sensei giving an Iai clinic at my dojo in the late 1980s.
He was one of the highest-ranking Iai senseis in Japan (9th Dan).

Shogo K. Sensei—Mu-Gai-Ryu kata. Houston, Texas Dojo.

Sadoyuki Kobayashi Sensei (left) and Harutane Chiba Sensei (right).

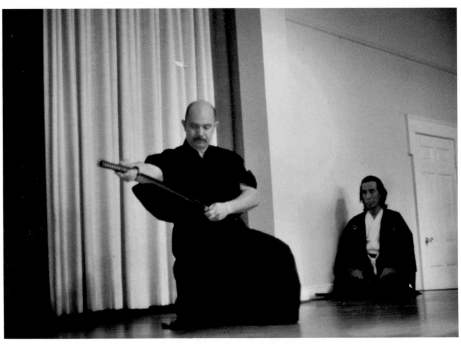

The author and Harutane Chiba Sensei at a Japanese festival.

The wavy *hamon* temper line shows the edge of the clay application
to the *mune* during the hardening process. Dmity Trush/Shutterstock.com

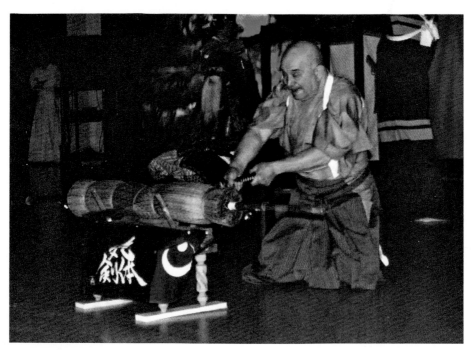

The author making a test cut.

Preparing to clean a sword. The red *uchiko* contains powdered *uchigumori* stone.
pedphoto36pm/Shutterstock.com

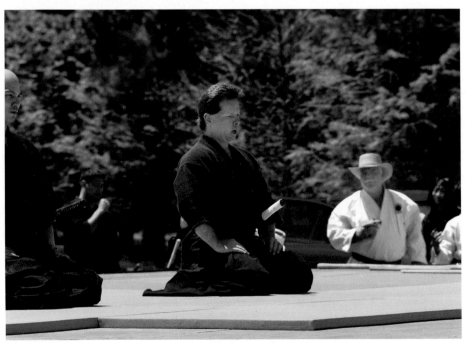

Steve T. in Sei-shin, the functions of the mind.

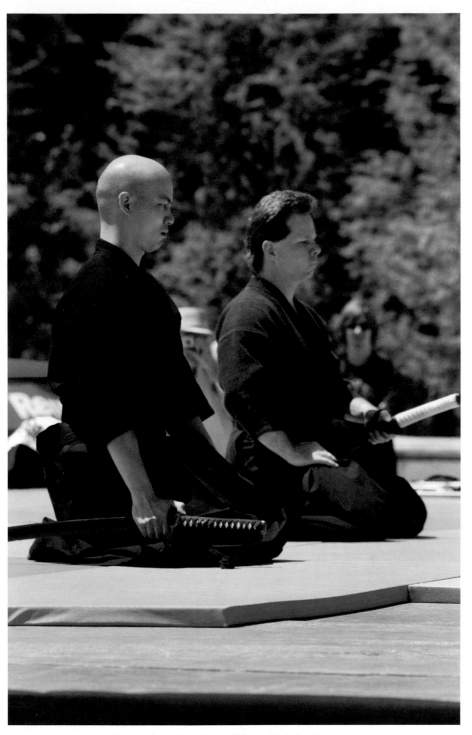

My students Ben H. and Steve T. sitting in seiza.

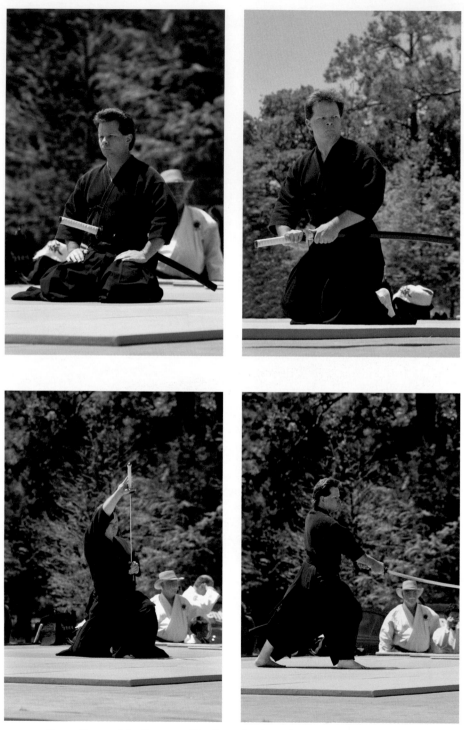

Above: Parts of the Japanese Kendo and Iado Federation kata Ukenagashi.

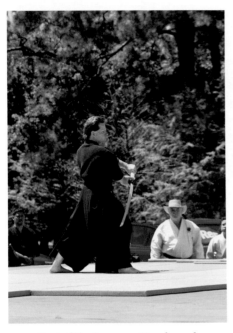

Part of the Japanese Kendo and
Iado Federation kata Ukenagashi.

Steve T. performing *chiburi*.

Steve T. performing Ippon Me Mae.

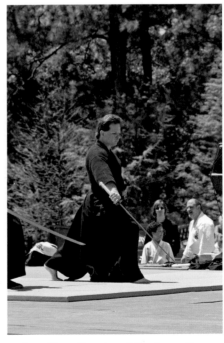

Steve T. performing *chiburi*, standing.

Above and opposite: Claudia Smith and the author performing a kata from the Katori Shinto Ryu using Kotori Ryu Boku-to or Ki-dachi swords.

Above and opposite: Koga Sensei and the author performing
an All Japan Kendo Federation kata.

An Iaidoka sitting in seiza. Per-Boge/Shutterstock.com

Fig. 105

Fig. 106

Fig. 107

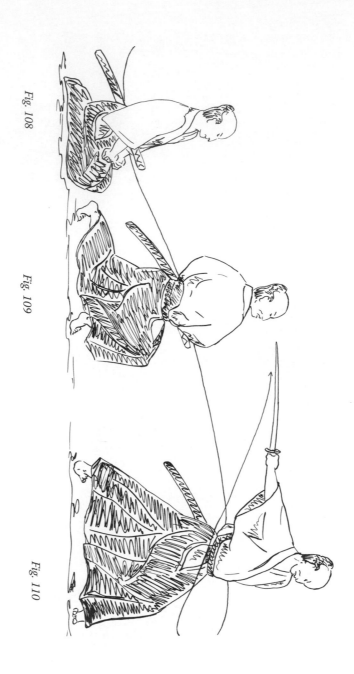

Fig. 108

Fig. 109

Fig. 110

Figures 108, 109, and *110* (opposite) show a standing cut from a sitting position. This is done by rising straight up, bringing your right foot forward, and then aligning your left foot to your right. Next, take hold of the handle and step out again with your right foot. Note in *Figure 110* that the right foot is positioned at a parallel angle with your body. The Bujutsu for this movement occurs when someone is standing over you and a few feet in front of you. You feel the intent of his attack and quickly rise, placing your right foot behind his front leg, squatting on your hips and putting pressure on his knee. This will cause him to fall backwards and allow you to make your cut successfully. Never take your eyes off of the opponent as you replace the sword into the saya. Step back with your right foot and resume the sitting position.

Figure 111 shows one way to perfect your timing and accuracy in Iai. You can start this exercise by having a friend toss up oranges or limes for you to use to make your cuts. Remember, go through each movement, and never leave out anything. The smallest movement is usually the most important. When you feel this is no longer a challenge, sit with your back to the thrower. Without a sound from either party, listen for the sound of the oranges leaving his hand and then turn and find your mark. I find sometimes when I practice alone, it is best to tie an apple on a string about head-high, letting the string swing back and forth. With my back to the apple, I turn and try to make the cut without cutting the string. When you get this down, try cutting the bottom of the apple and each time cutting only about ¼ of an inch at a time until only the stem is left. Another way to make the cut is to not let the apple swing; sit facing the apple and cut it in half on your first draw. Then on the second overhead cut, slice the apple

Fig. 111

again downward. It is important not to cut the string, but more important not to hit the apple with such force with the sword that you make it swing or break the stem. I must confess, however, with the prices of food these days, this can become expensive.

The least expensive way of practicing these cuts is to use a candle. Make yourself a small stand. I put four arms on my stand at different levels. Place a lighted candle on one of the arms and practice drawing and cutting off the flame. Do not cut the candle, just the wick so that the candle will go out. Do not knock the candle off of the stand. I once saw my master have such a stand with five candles, each candle was at a different level but all on a line going upward like a stairway. Sitting in the ready position very calmly, he rose to his feet making the draw. The next second there were only five small thin lines of smoke going to the ceiling. He held his sword in the air for a moment then replacing it in the saya he turned to me smiling and said, "I cannot train you in this way; I can only show you the way through these examples and watch you as you find your own path on the way."

Figures 112–114 show an Iai movement from the Japanese film *Sanjuro* in which Toshiro Mifune is surrounded by attackers. The Iai movement starts with a left-handed draw to the rear for a cut, then passing the katana over the right hand he finishes cutting the other two with a downward circle leaving only one against one. He then went into Kenjutsu—the Iai movement was finished with the second cut. These drawings help point out the difference between Iai Jutsu and Kenjutsu.

Fig. 112

Fig. 113

Fig. 114

Yato Uemoshichi Norikane (ronin of Ako)

CHAPTER NINE

Standing Iai Kata

Kata Number Five
Kesagiri
(Scapular Cut)

In this kata, you cut the enemy's armpit and then, with a downward diagonal cut, cut the left shoulder. Please remember that the same sword etiquette applies when you are standing as when you are sitting. Keep your back straight, left wrist close to your waist, and eyes on your opponent at all times.

Since we have come this far and are preparing for the last of the Japan Kendo Federation katas, I would like to relate another appropriate Zen story:

One day I asked the Sword Master, "How can I cut with the sword if I do not do it?" "It cuts," he replied. "I have heard you say that several times before, so let me put it another way, how can I wait for the cut to happen if I am no longer there?" He replied that it waits at the highest tension. "And who or what is this (it)," I asked? "Once you have understood that, then you will have no further need for me. And if I tried to give you a clue at the cost of your own experience, then I would be the worst teacher and would deserve to be sacked! So let us stop talking about it and go on practicing," he concluded. Then one day, after a draw with the sword, the Master made a deep bow and broke off the lesson. "Just then IT cut!" he cried, as I stared at him bewildered. And when at last I understood what he meant, I could not suppress a sudden whoop of delight. "What I have said," the Master told me, "surely was not praise, only a statement that ought not touch you. Nor was my sword meant for you, for you are entirely innocent of this cut. You remained this time absolutely without purpose in the highest tension, so that the cut fell from you like a ripe fruit. Now, go on practicing as if nothing had happened." "I am afraid I do not understand anything more at all," I answered, "even the simplest things have gotten in a muddle. Is it I who cuts with the sword, or is it the sword that draws me into the state of highest tension? Do I cut the goal or does the goal cut me? Is it spiritual when seen by the eyes of the spirit—or both or neither? Sword, goal, ego all melt into one another so that I can no longer separate them. And even the need to separate has gone. For as soon as I take the sword and cut, everything becomes so clear and straight-forward and so ridiculously simple." "Now at last," the Master broke in, "the sword edge has cut right through you."[1]

Always keep in mind there is much more to Iaido than meets the eye. Does the leaf leave the limb or does the limb leave the leaf? The point here is, do you control the drawing, or does the sword use you as a means of its self-expression? Remember, if you are having trouble with your Iaido at this point—stop. Go back and look at what you are doing. You may not be ready to continue yet. Do not be in a hurry to rush into deep water until you know how to swim: no one is drowning.

While you are moving forward in this first action, place your left hand on the saya and your right hand on the handle. Now turn the saya over so that the cutting edge is turned up. Push the sword guard forward with the thumb of your left hand. *(See Figure 115.)*

Stepping forward with the right leg, start the blade out of the saya. *(See Figure 116.)*

Fig. 115   *Fig. 116*

---

[1]   Eugene Herrigel, *Zen in the Art of Archery*. New York, NY: Pantheon Books, 1953
Author's Note: I have taken the liberty of substituting sword terminology for archery terminology in this passage.

When the right foot has completed its forward step, the blade should have completed its cut. The cut is made diagonally upward and your sword hand should stop its upward movement when it is about 20° upward from your right shoulder. *(See Figure 117.)*

Now without moving your feet or body, take hold of the sword handle with your left hand. *(See Figure 118.)*

Without moving your leg position, deliver a downward cut to the enemy's left shoulder. The hands should stop even with your navel. The ha of the blade should be turned about 15° outward and the kissaki, downward. *(See Figure 119.)*

Fig. 117

Fig. 118

Fig. 119

The next movement is to bring your katana to the hasso position while bringing the right foot to the rear. The hasso position with the katana means that you are in waiting for the enemy's next move. The tsuba will be in line with your chin. *(See Figure 120.)* Note that the hasso and right foot movements are done simultaneously.

Next, taking a step back with your left foot, place your left hand around the opening of the saya. Be sure that your wrist is against your waist. Now do chiburi (shaking the blood off of the blade). This is done by making an arc over your head and then bringing the blade downward. *(See Figures 121 & 122.)* Stop the blade's arc even with the angle of your right leg.

Fig. 120

Fig. 121

Fig. 122

Figure 123 shows the wrist bent while doing chiburi—this is incorrect.

The last movement in this as in all katas is to replace the katana in the saya. Bring the rear foot to the front foot while you are making the return and assume the taito shisei position. *(See Figure 124.)* Note that the taito shisei position is not shown. See Kata Ukenagashi (page 79).

Fig. 123

Fig. 124

Sugaya Hannojo Masatoshi

CHAPTER TEN

Multi-Directional Cutting

Kata Number Six
Morote-Suki
(Two-Hand Thrust)

Before we get into the last two katas of this ryu, I would like to point out again that Iaido is made up of two very important parts: technique and spiritual training. I feel that the spiritual aspect of the art is even more important than the technical. You must enter into the enemy's attack to defeat him, through his psychological weaknesses.

> This, what may be termed the "non-interfering" attitude of mind, constitutes the most vital element in the art of fencing as well as in Zen. If there is any room left even for the breadth of a hair between two actions, this is interruption. When the hands are clapped, the sound issues without a moment's deliberation. The sound does not wait and think before it issues. There is no mediacy here, one movement follows another without being interrupted by one's conscious mind. If you are troubled and cogitate about what to do, seeing the opponent about to strike you down, you give him room, that is, a happy chance for his deadly blow. Let your defense follow the attack without a moment's interruption and there will be no two separate movements to be known as attack and defense. This immediateness of action on your part will inevitably end in the opponent's self-defeat. It is like a boat smoothly gliding down the rapids; in Zen, and in fencing as well, a mind of no-hesitation, no-interruptions, and no-mediacy, is highly valued.[1]

I sometimes feel that when the marionette master puts his mind wholly into the play, his state of mind attains something of the swordsman's. He is then not conscious of the distinction between himself and the doll he manipulates. The play becomes really an art when the master enters into a state of emptiness. Some may see a difference between the marionette master and the swordsman because the latter's confronting a living personality who is aiming every movement at striking you down. But my

---

[1] D. T. Suzuki, *Essays in Zen Buddhism*, Foreword by Christmas Humphreys. New York, NY: Samuel Weiser, Inc. p. 363

way of thinking is different, in as much as both have realized the state of identity, it must operate alike regardless of individual objectives.

When the identity is realized, I as a swordsman see no opponent confronting me and threatening to strike me. I seem to transform myself into the opponent, and every movement he makes as well as every thought he conceives are felt as if they were all my own and I intuitively, or rather unconsciously, know when and how to strike him. All seems to be so natural.[2]

Starting this kata, Morote-suki, you are attacked from the front and rear. You cut the temple and thrust the solar plexus of the enemy in front of you. Then turning 180° to the rear, you deliver a downstroke to the enemy to the rear. After delivering this second cut, you turn back and deliver a final cut to the front.

Turning the saya so the ha is up, step out with your left foot and start your draw. *(See Figure 125.)*

Now, taking a second step with the right foot, finish the draw and cut the enemy's temple. *(See Figure 126.)*

---

[2] Ibid. pp. 205–204

Fig. 125

Fig. 126

Taking a chudan or center position with the sword (end of the handle at your navel and the point of the blade at the enemy's throat), place both hands on the handle and align the rear foot with the front. *(See Figure 127.)*

Moving the right foot forward, lower the tip of your sword to a level even with the enemy's solar plexus. *(See Figure 128.)* Note that you should stamp the right foot on the floor as you make this thrust.

Fig. 127

Fig. 128

As you center your left foot to the front foot, turn to the left, raising the katana over your head. (*See Figures 129 & 129A* for rear views of this move.)

Fig. 129

Fig. 129A

Now turn fully 180° to the rear and stepping out with the right foot and with the katana over the head, deliver a downward cut to the enemy's head. *(See Figure 130.)*

Now turning a full 180° back to the right, return to your starting position of the last move. The katana should be over your head as in *Figure 130*. You are now facing the first enemy. Deliver a downward cut to his head. Finish this movement as in *Figure 131*.

Without moving your feet, execute chiburi to the right side of your body. *(See Figure 132.)* Remember that the left hand moves the saya back. All other chiburi movements are the same as in previous katas.

Fig. 130

Fig. 131

Fig. 132

Kata Number Seven
Sanpogiri
(Three-Directional Cutting)

This kata starts out with the same movements as Morote-suki except that instead of turning the saya completely so that the ha of the blade is turned up, turn the saya only halfway. The ha is away from you. The action of this kata starts when you are faced with three enemies to the front, right and left sides. You will deliver three overhead cuts in succession: first the right, then the left, and lastly the final front cut.

Moving the left foot forward, take hold of the handle with both hands. Sensing the attack of the enemy on your right side, step with the right foot to the right drawing the blade with your right hand and make your cut on his right temple. *(See Figure 133.)*

Without moving your feet, look to the left and, pivoting on the balls of your feet, take hold of the handle with both hands and raise the katana over your head. Then turn. *(See Figure 134.)*

Fig. 133

Fig. 134

Now deliver a downward cut to the enemy on your left. Stop the blade in the chudan. *(See Figure 135.)*

Raising the sword as in *Figure 136*, again turn to the front using the balls of the feet.

Then, stepping with the right foot, deliver the third downward cut. *(See Figure 137.)*

Fig. 136

Fig. 135

Fig. 137

Stepping back with the right foot so the right foot is behind the left one, take the position with the katana called morote go-dan (sword overhead indicating zanshin spiritual defense). *(See Figure 138.)*

This position is usually held for a slow five count. Now step back with the left foot and place the left hand on the obi and saya. Then start your chiburi movement. *(See Figure 139.)* Be sure to arc the katana from your center to the right side of your body.

Fig. 138

Fig. 139

When the chiburi action is complete, take hold of the opening of the saya with your left hand. The left foot should still be in the rear. Then start your return. When the return is complete, bring the left foot to the right. Thumb on the tsuba and assume taito shisei standing. *(See Figure 140.)*

This completes the seven katas making up the Japan Kendo Federation Iaido. Remember that when the sword is properly handled, it helps us in an efficient way to contribute to the cultivation of the mind and spirit.

Fig. 140

Okuda Magodayu Shigemori (ronin of Ako)

CHAPTER ELEVEN

Bunkai of Iaido

The Inner Workings of Iai

Before we get into this chapter on the actual working movement of the art of Iaido, I must explain something. Sometimes it is hard for the Western mind to perceive that any martial art has a philosophy. But please keep in mind that the very use of the word Iaido and the wearing of the hakama with the Samurai sword are the marks of the adoption of the cultural heritage of the Japanese. All traditional arts from Japan are highly formalized and structured, often with rituals which to many outsiders may seem wasteful or superficial. To master any of these arts requires long years of training and most important, self-sacrifice.

Let your mind wander back to sixteenth-century Japan and read this story told by an old Zen master. This master's name was Konto-Okuda. Now, Konto was said to be the greatest Iai-Jutsu master of Japan during his time. Many students of the art tried to test their skills against him but none are said to have ever beaten him. Most were defeated long before their hands ever touched their swords. Konto was a man of about fifty years, not excessively large, but about average in build. He kept his head shaved to the point that the skin almost shined. He seemed to have an air of humility about him but a close look into his eyes sent a chill down your back. The thing most distinctive about him were the two swords that he carried. The saya were not of the high gloss we would expect, but more like the color of black charcoal. The sword guards were a little larger than most and the handles were wrapped in black cord. They engendered a mysterious feeling as did the man himself. And yet, deep inside, you could not but feel a warmth of understanding in him.

One day as the sun was slowly sinking behind the mountain and the chill of the evening was creeping upon the little monastery where Konto lived, a young man in his teens appeared at the outer gates. A Zen priest was lighting the gate lantern, when the young man asked, "Is this the monastery where Master Konto-Okuda resides?" Not stopping his duties, the priest pointed to a small door within the gates. The young boy bowed and started towards the door. Just as he was about to let his presence be known, the small door slid open. The young boy was startled for a moment, not knowing what to say. Then dropping to his knees the lad spoke, "Oh, please Master, you must teach me to be a master of Iai like yourself." The man in the door remained silent for a moment, which seemed like an eternity to the young man, but then as quickly as the door had opened, it shut.

As he stayed in this kneeling position, the boy could not believe his ears; the master had shut the door on him, Soto Mamoto, who had given up everything to seek out this Iai Master. Well, this just would not do; no one was going to shut a door in his face, master or not, without at least answering the question he had come so far to ask. Jumping to his feet, the young man quickly went up the two small steps and, knocking on the door, proclaimed in a loud voice, "You in there, who so rudely shut this door, I demand you come back out here and speak to me. I have but one question to ask you, and you will answer it before this night is through or my name is not Soto Mamoto."

The door slid open, as if by mysterious powers of its own. And there, out of nowhere, stood Konto-Okuda. As Soto looked into his eyes, he felt his knees starting to bend a little, and he knew it was not for the purpose of bowing. Looking deep into Soto's eyes, almost as if he were looking through him, not changing his facial expression or raising his voice, Konto said, "I hope your question is worthy of the answer." As Soto's head started to clear, he found himself on the ground in front of the small closed door. Lying there slowly moving his head from left to right, looking about, was convinced that he had been hit from behind. But to his surprise, he was all alone, with nothing but the flickering of the candle in the lantern at the front gate disturbing the stillness. He just could not believe it: one minute he was on the step and the next second on the ground. Now more than ever, Soto felt compelled to become the student of this man.

As the dampness of the evening dew crept into Soto's kimono there on the ground, it occurred to him to open the door and confront the master. But as he started to rise, his head hurt terribly and the thought of opening the door vanished.

Taking up a kneeling position in front of the steps, Soto waited. "The Master has to come through the door sooner or later," Soto surmised, "and when he does he will see how humble I have made myself. He will have to accept me as a student then."

Minutes turned into hours, and the hours brought the cold mountain night. Slowly his eyes started to close, and he fell into a deep slumber. When he opened his eyes, he felt the warmth of the morning sun on his back. Quickly looking up at the door, he saw that it was still shut. "Good", he thought, "he has not left yet and when he does, I will be waiting." Morning turned into afternoon and his legs began to ache. His back felt as if trampled by oxen, and his throat was parched. "Why does not the master come out?" he thought. "I do not know if I can stay here much longer." All at once there was an indescribable pain across his back. Again and again he felt a stick come crashing down upon him. As he tried to get to his feet to deflect the blows, he found his legs would not cooperate and he tumbled, falling flat upon his face. Then the blows changed from his back to his buttocks. He pulled with his arms, using all the strength left in his body until he was under the steps and safe from the madman. Looking through the steps at his attacker he saw Konto-Okuda shouldering a long piece of bamboo and laughing to the heavens. Konto's voice roared with laughter, "Where is this man who demands to ask me but one question? Could that be him I see under my house, he who demanded last night, and now acts like a dog and hides beneath my dwelling?" Then, as the words echoed, Konto went up the steps and Soto could hear the sliding of the door as it closed. Kneeling under the steps, trying to get the blood to circulate again in his legs, Soto could not help thinking to himself, "This man is stark raving mad, no wonder he is known as the greatest Iai-jutsu practitioner. A person would have to be mad to deal with such a man." Just then he heard the door slide open above him, and a torrent of water came pouring down upon him. "There, demanding-one with no manners, let me try to clean your outside while you do something with that which you call a brain."

That was enough. Out from under the steps Soto came. "Master" he shouted, "If you are not going to accept me as a student, then at least say so and I will be on my way." "Accept you?" Konto laughed, "You who came to me first demanding, then tried to show humility by kneeling all night outside my door, but was without humility enough to stay awake. Want you? No, I do not want you."

"So!" Soto broke in, "I will be on my way! Maybe I did start off on the wrong foot, and maybe I deserved the beating, but after all I have been through, don't you think you could at least answer my one question?"

Konto put his finger to the side of his nose and looked straight into Soto's face. For the first time Soto began to know fear. With a half-smile on his face but a frown upon his brow, Konto said almost in a whisper, "Tell me, little one, not that it really matters, what is your question?" Konto started down the steps, slowly placing his hand on the handle of his sword. "Come here so we can talk, little one." He was still moving forward towards Soto. Soto felt this was a dream, he could feel the master getting close, but he did not seem to see his body moving, Konto reached out with his right hand and grabbed the boy by his hair. "Now demanding one," Konto exclaimed, holding him so that his face looked straight into the afternoon sun, "Tell me what is this most important question?" Soto felt his neck was about to break and he knew he was either about to die or have his question answered. "What is this question, demanding one?" Konto said again softly, with eyes ablaze.

"Let go of my hair so I can stand up and I will tell you," Soto replied. Konto released his grip and it seemed to Soto like the hair on his head had grown a foot. Now Soto dropped to his knees at the master's feet and without looking up started to explain his question.

"Master, as I have said, my name is Soto Mamoto and I come from Kyushu. My father was the fencing master at Kumamoto Castle until he was killed by two ronin six months ago. It was at this time that I started on my journey to find you, Master." Konto broke in, "What was your father's name, little one?" "Shin No Fuji Mamoto," Soto replied. "Not Shin No Fuji Mamoto of Higo prefecture?" "Yes," Soto replied. Konto could scarcely believe it. Shin No Fuji and he had grown up together, fought side by side in the castle wars, got drunk together many times and eventually fell in love with the same woman. But he had not heard from his good friend in many years. Quickly, Konto's mind snapped back to the boy. "Tell me, little one, what was your mother's name? And is she not worried about her son so far away at a time she might need him most?" he demanded.

"Master, her name was Shimoke-Kuto, but she died when I was born and I only know of her from my father's uncle. My father would never let her name be spoken in his presence."

Konto reached down and put his hand under the boy's chin, lifting it so he could study the story on his face. Indeed, Konto thought, this is Shimoko's child. She was the most beautiful woman he had ever known and through this little one she still lived.

Just then a loud voice from the monastery gate cut short Konto's memories. The voice was so loud that it startled Soto, and he jumped to his feet. Konto reached out and pushed the boy to one side behind him. Two men standing at the gate moved toward him. Konto placed his hands inside his kimono, and turned to face them, and spoke, "My name is Konto-Okuda. What do you seek here?" One of the men replied, "We do not wish to hurt you, old man, we have come for that one, there," and pointed at the little one. "And what do you wish of him, may I ask?" questioned Konto. "That is none of your business," answered the ronin. "But you see it is my business, smelly one, for the one you seek is my student and therefore I am responsible for all of his actions," Konto retorted.

The ronin laughed smugly, then turned back to Konto and said, "So, bold one, who is acquainted with the gods, you are responsible for this little one. Then I suggest that you make yourself ready to meet your responsibilities." Konto remained silent and let his body relax. He studied the ronin eyes, never changing his own expression nor removing his hands from under his kimono. As the ronin drew his katana, his swift hands became only a blur to Soto's eyes but more unbelievable to the boy was that the master's entire body became a blur to the ronin movement. With the quickness of a mountain cat, the ronin tried to block what his eyes could not truly see. But it was too late, for when the ronin finally realized that the sword was coming from the old man's saya, he had already felt the ha cutting deep into his flesh. The ronin tumbled dead at Konto's feet. Konto quickly turned to face the other ronin, but he had vanished as suddenly as the life which Konto had just taken. Now making a circle over his head with his katana and a snapping movement with his wrist, he removed the blood from the end of his sword. Before Soto's mind had digested this movement, the sword was back in its resting place. Soto's heart was pounding like the sound of an attack drum and finally realizing that it was over, he ran to Konto's side. Looking down at the dead ronin and then to the master, he began to weep. "Master, these were the Samurai who killed my father! As my father was dying, he told me of you, he said to come here and to become your student."

"Not now, little one," Konto interrupted, "We will have plenty of time later to talk about such things. We must take care of first things first. This lifeless body must be cared for and we must pray for his misguided soul. Now go to my room and try to rest while I take care of these matters."

It was late evening when Soto heard the master come in. He did not move from where he had been sleeping, but just lay there thinking how never before had he known such a man, such a great warrior, and he knew that the answer to his question was within reach.

When Soto awoke the next morning he could see the master making tea. Quickly going over to where Konto was, he knelt down and, taking the kettle from the fire, began to pour the master's tea. "If I am going to be your student, master, you must allow me to do my duties. A student does not sleep while his master makes tea."

"It is good you know such things," Konto smiled. As they sipped their tea and warmed their bodies by the fire, Konto broke the silence and said, "Well, little one, I feel it is time we had our talk. You have come all this way to ask a question, but I must warn you that some questions are better never asked, for once you ask and seek the answer, you will be drawn into the trap of life. The answer could lure you away from all things that now seem important. You may start on the endless circle I have traveled, and find only that the end is no end at all. The revenge you hold in your heart for this other man may only bear bitter fruit, that neither you nor anyone else will be able to digest. With these things in mind, you may ask your question."

Soto looked at the master for a minute reflectively, put his cup down and began to speak. "Master, before my father died he made me promise to avenge his death. But in a way, I do not understand. He said I would only be able to set his spirit at rest by finding the answer to the sound of one hand clapping. He said unless I truly find this answer, the ronin would surely kill me and my death would be of no purpose. He then told me of you and explained if there was anyone on earth who could help me with the problem, it would be you."

Konto, looking into his tea cup, could not help but smile to himself, for he knew now without a doubt what he had suspected all along. Shin No Fuji had sent the little one on an endless journey for his own safety. He knew Soto would never leave the monastery now until he had found the answer. The answer would take many years. By the time he knew the answer, he would have forgotten why it was so important in the first place.

Soto cleared his throat, and the master looked up. The boy continued, "Master, do you know the answer?"

"Oh yes, I know the answer, little one! But first let me ask you a question. Do you know the sound of two hands clapping?"

"Is it important to know the sound of two hands, Master?" Soto replied. Konto poured himself a little more tea. "Yes, I am afraid so, little one, before you get into the water, you must first learn to swim. Remember if you are going to be my student and search for the answer of one hand, I can only instruct you in the use of the sword, I cannot teach you, you must teach yourself. The sound of two hands clapping is one of the most vital elements in the art of Kenjutsu, as well as in Zen. Always remember, little one, when the hands are clapped, the sound is heard without a moment's deliberation. If there is any room left even for a breath of air between these two actions, there is interruption. The sound does not wait and think before it issues, one movement follows another without being interrupted by one's conscious mind. Do you understand this, little one?"

"I must confess, master, I do not think I do," Soto replied. "Well, do not worry about it now," Konto smiled, "we have plenty of time and you must start your duties before the morning wastes away."

Bunkai

In truly learning the Bunkai of swordsmanship, you must find your circle and know the enemy's circle. When you have done this let him enter your circle. You then must advance into his until you have become intertwined with his attack. Now there is not attack and counter, only attack. This movement in Zen is called:

Seizing the enemy's spear and using it as the weapon to kill him.[1]

Explaining this is very difficult, but in his movement of attack, for one second you become the attacker. If you think of defending yourself you will surely feel the cut of his sword, but if you rush forward under his attack, pressing your own attack, he will slowly be defeated. Remember there are only eight directions of attack and eight directions of defense. The diagrams on the opposite page illustrate this.

---

[1] Ibid. p. 96

Center of attacker's body

Sword points before attack

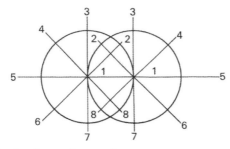

The attacker has begun his attack

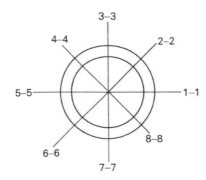

The attacker and defender have merged circles, leaving no attack or defense

Bunkai of Iaido

Starting with Ukenagashi kata, the following three illustrations will explain the actual movement of this kata or the bunkai. In the bunkai we are only interested in the three defending movements.

1. *Figure 141*: The enemy is sitting to your left and attacks you. Drawing your katana as the enemy steps with his left foot to make his attack, you turn your body just a little toward the attacker and block.
2. *Figure 142*: Rise to your feet, holding your katana in the previous blocking manner so that the enemy's sword slides down it and puts him off balance. Note: Do not forget to shift your feet. See the first paragraph on page 81 for the foot movement.

Fig. 141

Fig. 142

3.   *Figure 143*: Drawing the left foot back, make your cut to the enemy's left shoulder.

Note that returning the blade to the saya is not part of the bunkai. This is part of the kata. For further information refer to the Ukenagashi kata (page 79).

Fig. 143

Bunkai

Iaido-Hiza Kata-Tsuka-Ate has four movements, but I feel that the last strike is not Iai, but should be regarded as a separate sword cut. Therefore at my discretion I am only showing the first three movements as bunkai.

1.   *Figure 144*: The enemy in front attacks. Rise to meet the attack on your right foot and strike the attacker in the solar plexus with the butt of your katana handle.

Fig. 144

2. *Figure 145* shows that the first enemy has fallen, but you are now attacked from behind. Quickly pull the saya from the katana, which is done by moving your left hand back to your waist and leaving your right arm extended.

3. *Figure 146* shows you turning your upper body towards the attacker and thrusting into the enemy's solar plexus with the tip of your sword. To finish as in the kata, you would place the katana overhead and deliver a killing blow to the first attacker. Then you are again facing front and should slide one step forward with your right foot. For the katana's return, see Tsuka-ate Kata (page 93).

Fig. 145

Fig. 146

Bunkai

Tachi-Iaido Kesagiri bunkai has four movements.

1.   While you are walking, the enemy attacks you from the front. With your right foot forward, turn the cutting edge of your katana up and start your draw. *(See Figure 147.)*

     Figure 148 shows the blade on its way. If you study this drawing carefully you will note you are to be directly under the enemy's blade.

Fig. 147

Fig. 148

2.   Now the blade has made contact with the enemy's right armpit. This cut must continue until your hand is even with the enemy's right shoulder. *(See Figure 149.)*

3.   Take hold of the handle of your katana with your left hand and raise it to the right and above your head. *(See Figure 150.)*

Fig. 149

Fig. 150

4.   Without delay, deliver your final cut through the enemy's left shoulder. This should separate the top of his body from the bottom. *(See Figure 151.)* To make the return, refer to Kesagiri kata (page 119).

Fig. 151

Morote-Suki Kata (Two-Handed Thrust)

This kata includes two attackers, one in front and one in back. Taking one step with your left foot, place your hand on the handle of your sword. Now, taking a step with your right foot, draw your katana and cut the enemy with a Yoko (Side) Men. *(See Figure 152.)*

Fig. 152

Now taking a chudan (center position), bring the rear foot to the front. *(See Figure 153.)*

Now stepping out with the right foot and stamping it on the floor, make a double-handed thrust to the enemy's solar plexus. *(See Figure 154.)*

Fig. 153

Fig. 154

Bring the rear foot about 18 inches over to your left, pivot to the rear and raise the katana over your head. *(See Figure 155.)*

Your left foot should be forward. Next step with your right foot forward and deliver a downward cut to the enemy in the rear.

Pivoting on the balls of your feet, turn to the right 180° and raise the katana over your head. Step forward with your right foot and make your final downward cut to the first attacker. *(See Figure 156.)* Then, staying in the same position, execute chiburi.

Fig. 155

Fig. 156

Nakamura Kansuke Masatoki (ronin of Ako)

CHAPTER TWELVE

Sword Testing

We hear about sword testing, but to be truthful, anyone can take a sword and cut through Chinese polished mats. The real test with a sword lies within the person using the sword and their skill. If you look at the bottom photo on page 7 in the color section, you will see Japanese tatami covers rolled to make forty-one layers with a 2-inch bamboo pole down the center. This is soaked in water for three days, hung outside to dry, and then placed on a cutting stand with the ends tied down. Many people will say, "Okay, what's the big deal? I can cut through that easily." But the skill of the swordsman with this type of test, is to cut through the matting and bamboo to the last layer of tatami mat, not allowing the roll to be cut in half completely. If successful, the center will rise upward and you have formed "Mt. Fuji," as shown in the bottom-right photo on page 4 in the color section. I saw this demonstrated in Osaka, Japan in 1987; and it is particular type of sword testing that comes from the Japanese word *kaishaku*, meaning "learning his role in seppuku." See page 90, first paragraph, and *Figure 89 on page 91.*

When I think of testing the Japanese sword, I recall the legend of the great swordsmith, Okazaki Masamune. Masamune's swords are held in the greatest admiration by all sword collectors for their outstanding quality. The Muramasa sword made by one of his students was by no means something of lesser quality, but the master is said to have something divine in his sword that no other maker has ever been able to duplicate. The legend goes as follows:

> When someone was trying to test the sharpness of a Muramasa, he placed it in a current of water and watched how it acted against the dead leaves flowing down-stream. He saw that every leaf that met the blade was cut in twain. He then placed a Masamune, and he was surprised to find that the leaves avoided the blade. The Masamune was not bent on killing, it was more than a cutting implement, whereas the Muramasa could not go beyond cutting, there was nothing divinely inspiring in it.[1]

At the same time you must keep in mind this is only a Japanese legend and that even swords made by the same maker were made one at a time. Each sword was forged individually allowing possibilities for errors and, in some cases, flaws. These errors and flaws sometimes only show up in testing the blade. I am sure the swordsmith had many tests that he, or his assistants, conducted before the product of his unique craftsmanship was handed over to its prospective

---

[1] Ibid. p. 92

buyer. A sword made for the purpose of defending one's life in battle, and at times that meant cutting through heavy pieces of armor worn by the bushi. Therefore, most bushi would not accept a sword without subjecting it to a series of cutting tests that he or another Samurai who specialized in testing swords would perform. If the sword did not meet the highest of standards, it was discarded or melted down to make a spear or halberd. The Samurai who tested swords was licensed or appointed by the Shogun to execute condemned criminals. This allowed the use of live bodies for testing. The event was held with strict ceremonial formality. Witnesses were selected, special clothing was worn, and most importantly, upon conclusion all was recorded and a certificate was issued to certify the testing results. The sword tester then signed the nakago or tang of the sword in gold, giving the date, place, and whatever cut that he used against the victim and how many cuts were made.

There were, in addition, tests that did not require live bodies. But, before exploring that, I would like to explain the testing procedure from the beginning.

When a sword was to be tested, it had to be prepared by making a special handle for it. *(See Figure 157.)*

Fig. 157

This handle was made from two pieces of hard wood with adjustable holes (*mekugi*). The two metal bands around the handle slide up and down to assure a tight fit. Most professional testers carried their own testing handle which was made to his specifications.

There is much difference between doing Iaido and actually cutting something. As I have stated, it is almost impossible to learn Iaido to its fullest without knowing Kendo. Kendo teaches you the proper hand positioning along with the most vital cutting movements of the wrist action.

Proper Hand Position

The hand position shown in *Figure 158* is as follows:

1. Place the left hand on the handle so that the little finger is at the base of the kashira.
2. Let the fingers wrap around the handle so that the top of the kashira is about even with the back side of your wrist; place your index finger on the kashira.

    Note that the fourth finger is not wrapped around the handle. It balances the handle at the first joint from the end of the finger.
3. Now, place the right hand as shown in the diagram with the finger on the menuki.
4. Raise the sword over your head and make a downward cut, stopping the kashira even with your navel. The hands must twist around the handle while executing this movement as if wringing a wet towel.

Figure 159 shows the actual part of the blade that you cut with.

Fig. 158

Fig. 159

This reinforced part of the blade is called the *yokote*. All cuts with a katana must be made with the first 6–7 inches of the blade.

Figures 160 & 161 show the actual test cutting.

Fig. 160

Fig. 161

The setup can be accomplished by getting a piece of bamboo 3–4 inches in diameter, and a square or round pole about 4 feet in length and 7–8 inches in diameter. Bury the pole upright in the ground about half way. You can either drill out a hole in the top of the pole so that the bamboo will slide inside or you can drive a dowel into the top of the pole so that about ½ foot protrudes from the top. Now, place the bamboo over this dowel. You may even have to tie it to the dowel. When you have secured the bamboo and are ready to make the cut, you must keep these things in mind:

1.   Find the proper distance between you and the bamboo so that you will cut with only the first 6–7 inches of the katana.
2.   Decide which cut you will use. The heaven to earth cut shown in the diagram will be the easiest to start with.
3.   Make sure that your stance is correct. If you are cutting from right to left as in the drawing, your left foot is in the rear.

Note: *Remember to always keep the left leg in the rear.* This is very important because of the chance of an accident. If the cut is not clean, the blade may ricochet and cut your leg.

4.   Once you start your cut, it is absolutely necessary for you to follow all the way through. This will help to prevent a mishap due to a ricochet.
5.   Be sure to cut the bamboo at an angle. If you try to cut straight across, you might chip the ha or, more probably, just break the bamboo.
6.   The most important thing of all is to take this seriously. Make sure that you know what you are doing before you try it.

Another cutting test that is exciting is to cut through straw. After a straw bundle is prepared properly, it gives much the same feel as cutting the human body. This type of sword testing became popular after the Meiji prohibition of wearing the swords late in the 1870s. *(See Figure 162.)* The cut in the drawing would be the same as cutting through four bodies with one stroke.

To prepare the straw for this test is fairly simple:

1.   Select straw about 4 feet in length.
2.   Select a green piece of bamboo about 1½ inches in diameter and 2 to 3 inches longer than the straw.
3.   Roll the straw around the bamboo pole until you have a roll about 1 foot in diameter. Tie the ends and middle with a piece of cord.
4.   Take the bundle and soak it in a bucket of water. I find a large garbage can best suited for this purpose. The bundle must stay submerged in the water until the straw is completely soaked through, generally 24 hours.
5.   Now, remove the bundle and, using a high test cord (not rope or twine), wrap the bundle as tightly as possible so that the bundle is about 9 inches in diameter.
6.   Place the bundle in the sun until it is dry. This usually takes about a day and a half.

Fig. 162

When the straw is completely dry, it is ready for cutting.

Place the bundle on a wooden block as in *Figure 162*, tie the ends down, and you are ready to make your test.

If you do not wish to prepare a block of wood like that in the drawing, I find a wooden pine stool very suitable. Get a stool 3½–4 feet high with no back or armrests.

Place the bundle in the middle of the seat and tie the ends down to the supporting leg rungs. This cut involves only an overhead strike, as follows:

1. Determine your proper distance as in the previous test.
2. Place your feet apart, about 2 feet wider than your shoulders.
3. When you bring the katana down to make this cut, you must bend your knees slightly and push your ki down below your navel. Although this test seems fairly simple, I warn you that you will find it more difficult than you imagine.
4. Again, you must follow through mentally as well as physically to be successful.

Figure 163 shows a sword test using a piece of metal. I do not recommend this because you might destroy your katana.

Fig. 163

Human Body Testing

Figure 164 shows the arrangement used for human bodies. The body was laid on a mound of sand, face up so that the back was stretched tight. The cuts were made diagonally.

Fig. 164

Fig. 164A

Human testing was as often as not the case in medieval Japan. *Figures 165* through *168* show different ways that these tests were performed. Many times after the initial cut, the pieces were stacked up and cut again and again until there was not a piece of human flesh left larger than a hand.

Ni-Tai-Tai
Ni-Tari-qane
Ni-Chiwari
Ni-Wakiqa
Ni-Suritsuke
Ni-Ichi-No-Do
Ni-Ni-No-Do
Ni-San-No-Do
Ni-Kurumasnki
Ni-Rio Kuruma

Fig. 165

Tachiwari-Shimotatewari

Fig. 166

Two-body testing

Fig. 167

Ni-Rio Kuruma

Fig. 168

Figure 169 shows many of the test cuts and their names. *Figure 170* shows descending and lateral cuts of various angles and levels.

Fig. 169

Fig. 170

Hayami Tozaemon Mitsutaka (ronin of Ako)

CHAPTER THIRTEEN

Mu Gai Ryu Iai Hyo-Do

Mu Gai Ryu Hyo-Do is one of the older styles of Iai-Jutsu. I have been told by my master, Mr. Shiyogo Kuniba, a student in the art, that there are only two or three schools left in all of Japan that teach this particular style. Considering the style, I feel the only reason it has a "do" instead of a "jujitsu," is because of the era. Swords are no longer used for fighting, so to keep up with the modern age, we must change to the way it used to be. If we translate Mu Gai Ryu Hyo-Do, another question comes up. Does the "do" in the name actually mean a "way" like Kendo or has it always been a way? Translated, the name means "Empty self style or drawing of the leopard's way." It seems that no one is really certain just how the style's name came about. Master Kuniba's father handed it down to him when he was just a young boy. The style had been known to only a small clan of bushi in the southern part of Japan, around Shimonoseki.

Some of the outstanding characteristics of the style are:

1. Drawing starts when seated on your heels, with the balls of your feet on the floor instead of your insteps.
2. Every return of the blade ends with you in the sonkyo position and then going to tachi.
3. Instead of the back of the blade coming in front of your body as in the Japanese Kendo Federation style, in Mu Gai Ryu Hyo-Do, it comes from the side of the shoulder in a horizontal position.
4. The most outstanding difference between this style and any other is the that you change the position of your feet with each cut. Some have said that this makes the style slower when delivering the second cut. To this I have no comment for I am but a student in the art, and not a master. Nevertheless, this extra movement does make you combine sword and body, so I feel that it has merit.

The complete style has twenty-four katas, twelve sitting and twelve standing. There are also twelve tsuka wazas and several saya wazas. It would be too involved to introduce you to all these at this time, so I have picked the katas and wazas that I feel would be appropriate at a beginner's level. These will consist of seiza kata, one tachi kata, several tsuka wazas and one saya waza. You will notice that I have chosen to use the bunkai to illustrate Mu Gai Ryu Iai Hyo-Do. I feel that this will help you to understand the movements more clearly.

You must keep in mind when practicing this ryu that it was practiced in Japan when Iai was a true way of life. It will help you obtain insight through intensive training within the old ryu-ha, where the true spirit of the art is fully manifested.

Mu Gai Ryu Hyo-Do

Za-Iai-Seiza katas

1.	You	Useful
2.	Shin	Truce
3.	Tsuka-Waza	Handle Technique
4.	Yoko Tsuka Tomoe	Side Handle Circle
5.	Te-Saya Waza	Hand Saya Technique
6.	Muchi-no-Kimo-Shippo	Lashing Tail
7.	Ten Te	Heaven Hand

Other Mu Gai Ryu Hyo-Do katas I have not included in this printing:

1.	Ren	Training
2.	Sa	Difference
3.	Hibiki	Sound
4.	Hibiki Kaeshi	Sound Return
5.	Go	Friendship
6.	Zen-Go-Sen	Forward Backward Offense
7.	Ma-Ko (Ma-Tsu-Ko)	Right in Front
8.	Karatake	Empty

Kata Number One
You-Seiza
(Useful Sitting)

1. As you feel the intent of the enemy's attack, look into his eyes. Sit on your heels with the balls of the feet on the floor. Do not move, but stay as relaxed as possible. Keep your hands on your thighs. *(See Figure 171.)*

Fig. 171

Fig. 171A

Fig. 172

2.   Let the enemy start his attack. Rise on your knees using your thigh muscles. Now, take hold of your katana, bring your right leg forward, and block the enemy's draw with the tsuka of your katana. *(See Figure 172.)*
     Note: *Figure 171A* shows a close-up of this movement of pushing downward with the tsuka on the enemy's wrist, preventing him from completing his draw. Please notice that the thumb is on the tsuba.

Push forward now with your katana keeping a downward pressure on the enemy's wrist, forcing him down and backward. *(See Figure 173.)*

Fig. 173

3.   The katana has now cleared the saya, and as you position it over your head the enemy again starts his attack. *(See Figure 174.)*

Fig. 174

4. Sliding forward about one-half foot with the right (forward) leg, deliver a downward cut, cutting the head, solar plexus, and the right wrist. *(See Figure 517.)*

Fig. 175

5. Chiburi: Bring the right leg back, step out with the left leg and make a circle over your head with the katana. Note that these two actions are done simultaneously. The shaking of the blood from the katana is like that of the Japan Kendo Federation's Iaido Kata Number One except that you do not stand up. Stop the blade at a 45° angle. *(See Figure 176.)*

Fig. 176

6.   To replace the katana in the saya, place your left hand around the opening of the saya extending your thumb and index finger. Bring the back of the katana just below the tsuba between them. The tip of the blade will be pointing up and slightly over your left shoulder. *(See Figure 177.)*

Fig. 177

7.   As you slide the katana down through your thumb and index finger, push your right hand outward. Slide the front foot back to the rear foot, immobilize the waist and keep the right knee on the floor. The tip of your blade should now be at the opening. Note that these two actions must move as one: blade and front foot move together. Starting the katana in the saya so that it rides on its back, cutting side up, take the sonkyo position on the balls of the feet with the right knee on the floor. Your legs will be a 90° angle, your back straight, and your eyes looking at the attacker. As the blade comes to a stop, place your thumb on the tsuba and sit firmly on the balls of your feet. *(See Figure 178.)*

Fig. 178

8. Tachi: Bring the left knee forward with the right knee remaining on the floor. Take your hands off of the katana and saya and place them on your thighs. Hold this position for about a three count. Now, replace your left hand on the saya with the thumb on the tsuba. Take your right hand and place it on the kashira. Then slide your left foot forward and rise to your feet. Your left foot will be forward. Next, bring back your left foot to the right foot and align them. Assume tachi. Note that the tsuba will be positioned at your navel. Keep the sword in a horizontal position. Prepare for the next action.

Kata Number Two
Shin-Seiza
(Truce in Sitting)

1. While sitting on your heels with the balls of the feet on the floor, knees about one and a half feet apart, back straight, head erect and looking straight into the opponent's eyes, you sense his intent to attack you.
2. Placing your left hand on the saya, turn the saya so that the blade is pointing down. Place your thumb on the tsuba and push so that the habaki is exposed. *(See Figure 179.)*

Fig. 179

3.   Now the attacker makes his actions clear. You push the tsuka across your body to the right and take hold of it, but do not expose your wrist. *(See Figure 180.)*

Fig. 180

4.   Make your draw, moving your right foot forward, stamping it on the floor. Remember that you do not lean forward and that you use your thigh muscles to rise straight up. Next, move your right foot. The finish of the draw and the stamping of the foot must come at the same time. The draw stops with the wrist even with the top of your head. Note that the attacker counters by returning to seiza and reclining. *(See Figure 181.)*

Fig. 181

5.   Now, place the katana over your head as in *Figure 182.* Note that the attacker has lost his balance and has started to fall backwards.

Fig. 182

6.   Starting your downward cut, change feet and bring the right leg back and advance the left. As the downward cut is completed, the attacker's wrist falls off. *(See Figure 183.)* Note that you will advance forward about one foot with the changing of the legs. The balls of the feet are on the floor. The chiburi and sword return are the same as in the previous kata.

Fig. 183

Kata Number Three
Tsuka Waza
(Handle Technique)

This is just one of the many tsuka wazas in Mu Gai Ryu Iai Hyo-Do. I have included it for the sole purpose of letting you see the versatility of the style.

1.   Sitting side by side with the attacker on your right, the attacker starts his draw. You rise straight up using your thigh muscles. *(See Figure 184.)*
      Next, you step out with the left foot slightly forward toward the attacker. Place your hands on your katana and start to make your draw.

2.   Instead of drawing the blade all the way out of the saya, stop about half way, placing the tsuka on the attacker's tsuka, forcing him to return to seiza. *(See Figure 185.)*
      Note that *Figure 184A* shows a close-up of this movement. After you have stopped their attack, return to seiza.

Fig. 184

Fig. 184A

Fig. 185

Kata Number Four
Yoko-Tsuka-Tomoe
(Side Handle Circle)

1. The attacker has caught you unaware and has advanced his attack before you can counter with a draw of your own. *(See Figure 186.)*
2. As the attacker takes advantage of your surprise, you fall backwards and to the right, using your right hand to catch your balance. Placing the left hand on your saya, thumb on the tsuba, pull the saya forward about 2 feet. *(See Figure 187.)*

Fig. 186

Fig. 187

Fig. 188

3.   The attacker now feels he has the full advantage of his attack for a "men," or head cut. You have now pulled the saya far enough out that the tsuba is even with your chin. *(See Figure 188.)*

4. As the attacker makes his downward cut, you block it using the tsuka of your katana. *(See Figure 189.)*

Fig. 189

Fig. 190

5. When the enemy's blade makes contact with your tsuka, start coming to the seiza position, keeping tension on his blade.
    Make a small circle to your left, holding his blade down enabling him to withdraw his katana. *(See Figure 190.)*

6.   You have now resumed your seiza position. Move your right leg forward and pull the saya, attacking the enemy just under the chin with the tsukagashira of your katana. Note that your right knee will be in front and centered with the attacker's body. Keep your back straight and lock your elbows with the strike, then relax. *(See Figure 191.)*

Fig. 191

Fig. 192

7.   Keeping your attack flowing, leave the right hand extended and pull the saya from the blade. The saya will return to the obi so that it will maintain its original position. *(See Figure 192.)*

8. As you withdraw the attack at the enemy's chin, he changes his leg position and tries to counter. You quickly raise your katana over your head. Also change the position of your feet and slide about 12 inches forward. The left leg is now forward and the back of the blade is resting between the thumb and index finger over the head. *(See Figure 193.)*

Fig. 193

Fig. 194

9. Using your left hand to guide and apply extensive pressure, bring your katana down in a circle in front of you, striking the enemy. *(See Figure 194.)*

10.   Stop your attack when the tsuba is even with your waist and the kissaki of your katana is at the attacker's waist. *(See Figure 195.)*
11.   Execute chiburi as in the previous katas.
12.   Execute *kaeshi* (return of katana to saya) the same as in the previous katas.
13.   Execute tachi the same as in the previous katas.

Fig. 195

Kata Number Five
Te-Saya-Waza
(Hand Saber Technique)

1.   Sitting beside you, the enemy starts his attack. Quickly reach over with your right hand and pull upwards on his saya. Your left hand simultaneously goes to your saya, thumb on the tsuba. *(See Figure 196.)*

Fig. 196

2. While still pulling upward with your right hand, pivot on your left knee and bring your right leg forward. *(See Figure 197.)*

Fig. 197

3. Your attacker has now lost his balance. Continue your own attack by taking hold of your own katana and trying to strike him in the face with the tsukagashira. *(See Figure 198.)*

Fig. 198

4.   The enemy has fallen back still further avoiding your tsukagashira attack. Now, bring your right leg back and step forward, gaining about one foot with your left leg. Deliver an overhead downward cut to the attacker's neck. *(See Figure 199.)*

5.   Chiburi, kaishi, and tachi are repeated as in previous katas.

Fig. 199

Kata Number Six
Muchi-no-Kimo-Shippo
(The Lashing Tail)

It might be well to note here that this kata might have been the origin of the style's name. I must admit that when I have shown this particular kata to others in the art of Iai, they are somewhat surprised. I do not mean to imply they have not seen it before, but I feel they are surprised that a Westerner would know about it.

1.   The enemy attacks with sword already drawn. You quickly turn your saya with your left hand so that the cutting edge is pointing downward and take hold of the tsuka with your right hand. *(See Figure 200.)*

2.   Pivoting on your right knee and bringing your left leg to a 90° angle to your right will move you across and in front of the attacker. This action allows your saya to connect with the attacker's leading knee and turn his body to the left and off balance. Note that as you are pivoting, you should pull the katana from the saya so that the back of the blade is towards you. *(See Figure 201.)*

Figure 201A is a close look at the saya position. The saya must hit the attacker in the bend of the knee and even with the knee cap.

Fig. 200

Fig. 201

Fig. 201A

3.   While the enemy is trying to regain his balance and counter your attack, thrust into his solar plexus with the tip of your katana. The blade is perpendicular to the floor. You do not move the lower part of your body, but pivot from the waist up for the thrust. *(See Figure 202.)*

Fig. 202

4.   The attacker has now fallen backwards with the thrust. Moving the left leg back to your left, placing the katana over your head, and sliding forward using your left foot, deliver a downward stroke to the enemy's left wrist. *(See Figure 203.)*

5.   Chiburi, kaeshi, and tachi are repeated as in the previous katas.

Fig. 203

Kata Number Seven
Saya-Ushiro
(Behind)

1. When you are attacked from behind while in the seiza position, listen for the katana coming from the saya and the rustle of cloth as the enemy makes his attack. *(See Figure 204.)*

Fig. 204

2. Stepping forward with your right foot, take hold of your katana with your right hand. Place the left hand on the saya and turn the edge of the blade upwards. Pull the katana straight forward and upward. The tsukagashira is pointing upward and the kissaki towards the floor. The katana is still on your left side with the right arm across your body and forward. *See Figure 205*, which shows the beginning of this movement.

Fig. 205

3.   Holding the katana perpendicular to the floor, bring it across to the right side of your body and thrust the kissaki behind you. This is done with the hamon pointing upwards and the blade kept close to your right side. Now, pivoting the top part of your body, extend your arm behind you and thrust to the enemy's solar plexus. *(See Figure 206.)*

Fig. 206

4.   Bringing your right leg back so that both knees are on the floor, and with your back still facing the enemy, pivot on your left foot 180°. Step forward with your right leg again. You are now facing your enemy. Take hold of the mune with the palm of your left hand and push upward against the enemy's left wrist. *(See Figure 207; Figure 207A* is a closer view of this action.)

Fig. 207

Fig. 207A

5. Let the back side of the katana swing down beside your right leg and twist your right wrist, taking hold of the tsuka with your left hand over your head. Allow the tsuka to pivot in the palm of your right hand. Raising the katana high, almost to arm's length, prepare for your downward stroke. *Figure 208* shows completion of the downward cut.

Fig. 208

6.   Execute chiburi in the same manner as the previous katas.
7.   *Figure 209* shows the start of kaishi, and *Figure 210* shows the finish.
8.   Execute taichi in the same manner as in the previous katas.

Fig. 209

Fig. 210

Kata Number Eight
Ten-Te
(Heaven Hands)

1. As you are walking, an enemy pulls your katana from the saya and tries to strike you with it. You immediately extend your right hand. The palm is inward. Next, step out with your right foot. *(See Figure 211.)*

2. When the enemy starts to attack, take hold of the tsuka from the bottom side by placing your right hand between his hands. Next, pivot on the ball of the right foot and step behind the right leg with the left and turn 180° counter-clockwise. *(See Figure 212.)*

Fig. 211

Fig. 212

3.   Constantly pressing forward with your right hand to prevent the enemy from regaining his balance, step across in front of his knees with your right foot, forcing him to press his stomach against your right hip. Keeping the cutting edge of the katana away from you, make a circle with your right hand and bring the katana to your right hip. Simultaneously, lift your right leg, as in Judo's harai-goshi. Before the enemy hits the floor, place your left hand on your saya. *(See Figure 213.)*

4.   Now, pulling the tsuka from his hands, place the kissaki in the koikuchi, starting the return. *(See Figures 214 & 215.)*

Fig. 213

Fig. 214

Fig. 215

Kata Number Nine
Chiba Hokushin-Ito-Ryu
(Two-Man Kata with Wakizashi)

1. The attacker on the left with a katana is attacking the defender on the right with a wakizashi (short sword). The distance is greater with the katana. *(See Figure 216.)*

Fig. 216

2.   The attacker steps forward with his right foot, drawing his katana. The defender, feeling the pressure and realizing he is too far away to use his short sword, steps across his body with his left foot and reaching towards the floor with his right hand downward starts a forward rolling fall, taking a hold of his short sword with his left hand. *(See Figure 217.)*

Fig. 217

3.   The attacker brings his rear foot up to his right foot, sword drawn and starts to tsuku at the defender's throat. Defender reaches out with his right hand towards the floor. *(See Figure 218.)*

Fig. 218

4.   The attacker steps forward with his right foot, bringing the tsuku to his waist, keeping the sword tip up thrusting forward with his hands. The defender continues his rolling forward. *(See Figures 219 & 220.)*

Fig. 219

Fig. 220

5. The attacker brings his rear foot forward, seeing the defender starting to recover from his rolling motion, steps back with his left foot, keeping his sword in the center of his body. *(See Figures 221–223.)*

Fig. 221

Fig. 222

Fig. 223

6.   The defender steps forward in a kneeling position with his right foot, drawing his short sword, blocking the thrust of the attacker's sword while pushing the attacker's sword to the right (defender's left). *(See Figures 224–226.)*

Fig. 224

Fig. 225

Fig. 226

7. The attacker takes advantage of this pushing movement and brings his sword to his right side then quickly cuts at the defender's knees. The defender jumps upwards avoiding the attacker's cutting actions. *(See Figures 227–229.)*

Fig. 227

Fig. 228

Fig. 229

8.   The defender, upon landing, brings his short sword to his right hip, quickly steps forward with his left foot, and placing his left hand on the attacker's upper right forearm, keeps him from moving his katana from his left side. *(See Figures 230–232.)*

Fig. 230

Fig. 231

Fig. 232

9.   The defender keeps pushing on the attacker's forearm, slightly pushing in a leftward direction while keeping his short sword in a ready position at the attacker's solar plexus. The attacker uses his rear right foot to regain his balance and comes to a standing position. They both take the chudan-no-kami distance, perform noto and both bow. *(See Figures 233–235.)*

Fig. 233

Fig. 234

Fig. 235

Kataoka Gengoemon Takafusa (ronin of Ako)

CHAPTER FOURTEEN

Kenjutsu Kata

I have included the Ipponme kata, or the First Kata of the All Japan Kendo Federation, in this book to show you the difference between Iaijutsu and Kenjutsu. Because there is some debate on the issue, I cannot say with certainty whether or not the katas in Kendo are Kenjutsu. But two of my sensei agree that they are, so I must concur.

Figure 236—Ya (the attacker) and *tow* (the defender), kneeling opposite each other, katana on the right side with the cutting edge away from them.

Fig.236

Figure 237—Ya and tow, bowing to each other, presenting their right hands to the floor first.

Fig. 237

Figure 238—Taking hold of their katana with the right hand, thumb on the tsuba and cutting edge up, then rise, using the right leg. Next, facing the flag or honored guest, bow from the waist.

Fig. 238

Figure 239—Without moving the sword position, each man turns his back on the other and takes nine steps, turns to face the other and bows. They now place the katana on their left sides, sliding it through their obi, cutting edges up, thumb still on the tsuba and feet together.

Fig. 239

Fig. 240

Figures 240 & 241—Both ya and tow start out at the same time using their right feet and take three steps forward. All this time they maintain eye contact. They now assume the sonkyo position.

Fig. 241

Figure 241 shows the drawing of the swords. The first 5–6 inches of the tip of their blades must cross and the point of the blade point at one another's neck.

Figure 242—They rise to a standing position, keeping their chudan or center position and placing their left feet to the rear. They now lower the tips of their swords so that each man's sword is pointing to the left knee of his partner. Holding this position and starting with the left foot, each man takes five steps to the rear, keeping eye contact at all times.

At this ten-step interval, each man brings his katana to the chudan (center) position. After holding this position for about a five count, they are now ready to start the kata.

Fig. 242

Fig. 243

Ya on the left brings his katana to the jodan position as well but does not move his feet. Tow's right foot is still leading. *(See Figure 243.)*

They now take three steps forward, ya starting with his left and tow with his right foot. This will bring them close enough to the chudan position that the tips or *kensen* would meet.

In this jodan position *(Figure 243)*, ya makes his attack by stepping forward with his right foot and delivering a head or *shomen* cut to tow. He stops the cut about even with tow's right knee. *(See Figure 244.)* Tow, sensing ya's attack and reacting at the moment, starts his movement. Tow steps back with his left (rear) foot one step, letting the right foot follow naturally. He simultaneously shifts his hands backwards slightly. This movement allows ya's sword to pass in front of him and he evades the cut.

Ya now steps forward with his front right foot and delivers his own shomen cut. *(See Figure 244.)*

Fig. 244

Fig. 245

Figure 245—Ya lowers the tip of his sword so it is pointing to tow's rear foot in the gedan position, while taking one step back with his left foot. Tow advances one step forward with his left foot, keeping the kensen of his katana to the center of the attacker's face.

Fig. 246

Tow now takes one step to the rear with his left (front) foot and assumes the jodan position. *(See Figure 246.)* Note that Ya stays perfectly still while tow is performing this move. He does, however, maintain eye contact.

Ya and tow now assume chudan position. *(See Figure 7.)*

Then, both men lower the tips of their katana. *(See Figures 247 & 248.)*

Beginning on the left foot, each man takes five steps to the rear. This concludes the Ipponme kata.

Fig. 247

Fig. 248

Ohishi Kuranosuke Yoshitaka (ronin of Ako)

CHAPTER FIFTEEN

Chushingura

The Story of the Loyal Forty-Seven Ronin
"The Treasury of Loyal Retainers"

One of the most-often told and well-known Samurai stories in all of Japan is *Chushingura* or in English, *The Forty-Seven Ronin*. Now *ronin* literally means "wave man" or "one who is tossed up on the endless sea." He has no master; therefore he comes and goes endlessly. In 1701, in the month of February, there lived a Samurai by the name of Asano Takumi-no-Kami, who was the lord of Ako Castle. This was a time in Japanese history when the people enjoyed absolute peace and the country grew in wealth and prosperity. The militaristic spirit was nearly gone. The Shogun, who ruled all of Japan, had become more interested in luxury than in tradition, and most of the Japanese people followed his example, all that is, except the brave military Samurai. The spirit of bushido still lived in their hearts.

The Mikado sent an Imperial ambassador to Tokyo. Asano Takumi-no-Kami and Kamei-Sama were expected to receive and entertain the ambassador and his party. These two lords were not experienced in the proper procedure for entertaining such nobility, so they sought out a man by the name of Kozuke-no-Suke, who they knew was well versed in these matters and for many years had taken part in these types of receptions. Now Kozuke-no-Suke was a man of greed and unbeknownst to Asano, Kamei-Sama had bribed Kozuke to provide him with good advice. Asano was a Samurai of great honor and the notion of bribery never entered his mind. After not receiving any kind of payment from Asano, Kozuke grew angry and repeatedly made fun of Asano, causing him to make mistakes. One day when Asano was taking instructions, Kozuke proclaimed, "Asano, you are nothing but a village fool. Here, let me find something more suited to your wits. Tie the cord of my hat." To this, Asano could hold his temper no longer and drew his short sword and attacked Kozuke, cutting him upon the head. Kozuke ran down the hall in fear of his life with Asano in pursuit. Catching Kozuke, Asano again struck out with his short sword, this time cutting the shoulder. Just as he was about to deliver the finishing blow, a Samurai by the name of Kajikawa Yosobie caught Asano from behind and wrestled him to the floor, allowing Kozuke to make good his escape. As soon as Kozuke was safe and his wounds attended, he ordered the arrest of Asano for the attempt

Asano attacking Kozuke

on his life. According to the law, just the drawing of a sword in the Shogunal Court was a capital offense. So Asano was immediately given over to Tamura-Ukyo-Dayu, Lord of Shinoseki in Mutsu, a small suburb of Tokyo, to await the results of a deliberation of his offense. The decision came that very afternoon, an unusually swift verdict; Asano was ordered to commit seppuku immediately. He was taken to a small garden in the courtyard, where inspectors and seconds were appointed on the spot.

As Asano stepped upon the mat, the place for the ceremony, he asked for paper and pen. This was brought to him without delay and he composed a poem which read:

Frailer far than the tender flowers
That are soon scattered by the wind.
Must I now bid a last farewell
And leave the general spring behind?

With this he laid down the writing material, lowered the top of his kimono, tucking the sleeves under his knees and committed seppuku.

Outside the gate of Kozuke Castle there awaited a Samurai by the name of Kataoka-Gengoyemon whose job it was to accompany his lord Asano to and from the castle each day. Upon hearing of his lord's sentence and demise, he immediately ran back to his lord's quarters in the city and reported the news of Asano's death to Kayano Sempei and Hayami Tozayemon, two of Asano's retainers. They in turn made their way to Ako Castle, which in those days was a four and a half day's journey. When they arrived, Kayano reported immediately to Ohishi, the head Samurai at the Castle.

"Ohishi!" Kayano shouted, "We have failed our Lord Asano. He was sentenced to seppuku four days ago for attacking Lord Kozuke in the palace. Kill me Ohishi, I beg you. I am not trustworthy."

Ohishi, lifting him by his kimono from his knees to his feet, shouted, "What do you mean Asano is dead? Tell me again, you worthless peasant, tell me and stop your whining like a woman." As Kayano tried to explain with tears running down his cheeks, Ohishi hit him with all his might. "You were sent to protect our Lord Asano and this is how you repay his kindness," said Ohishi, looking down on the floor where Kayano lay, "I should take your worthless life here and now." Ohishi reached for his sword and Kayano, remaining prostrate, jerked back his kimono so that his neck would be exposed to the blow of the oncoming katana. But to his surprise, the blow did not fall. When he finally looked up he could see that Hara Sayemon and Oishi Sezayemon had joined Ohishi, and they were trying to explain the exact circumstances that had culminated in seppuku for their lord.

Ohishi slowly slid his katana back into his saya and told the two men to gather all the retainers in the castle for a meeting in the Pine Corridor. Then Kayano saw Ohishi looking at him, and he again extended his neck. But instead of the sword's edge, Kayano felt a warm hand on his shoulder. Turning his head upward, Kayano saw a firm but smiling face looking down upon him. "Kayano, I know how you feel and I am truly sorry for the harsh words I spoke," Ohishi said, "But now I have an important mission for you." Lifting Kayano to his feet, he continued, "I want you to go to Teppozu Castle near the river Sumida and tell our lord's wife what has happened this day. Quickly reaching into his kimono, Ohishi gave Kayano some coins and bid him a speedy return. Then turning, he started towards the Pine Corridor, knowing he must break the news to the awaiting Samurai.

When Kayano arrived at Teppoza Castle, it was only to find that his lord's wife had already received the news of her husband's death and had shaved her head that very day in preparation to become a nun under the name of Yozei-in. She would spend the rest of her years praying for her departed husband's soul. More important, Kayano thought to himself, was the news that Kira Kozuke-no-Suke had sent word to his father-in-law at the Imperial Castle of what had happened. He was sure that Asano's retainers would take reprisal on him for the death of their lord, so he requested as many Samurai as could be spared to come to his aid. With these extra warriors he could withstand the oncoming attack.

Asano composing his death poem

With this most important information, Kayano remounted his horse and headed back to Ako Castle. Kayano kept thinking to himself as he raced through the still night, "I must not let my lord down again. If there is going to be a battle as Kozuke-no-Suke suspects, I must not be late. This time I will run under each sword of my lord's enemies and kill until I am killed." He could not help smiling to himself as he lashed out with his small whip. "Faster and faster, you brave and noble horse, take me faster. I must not be late this time."

When he arrived at Ako Castle, it was late afternoon of the fourth day. He saw no one and a chill grew into a cold sweat across his body. "No," he thought, "they have gone! How could they leave without me?" Just as he was dismounting, there came a most welcome sound to his ears, Ohishi Kuranosuke's voice. "Well Kayano, I see that you have returned to us. How did our lord's wife receive the news?" Kayano quickly related everything that had taken place, being sure not to omit any small details. "Well done Kayano, yes, well done indeed." Ohishi replied.

To this Kayano replied, "What decision have you reached on the revenge of our lord?" Ohishi reached up and ran his hand over the top of his head. He stopped with his hand over his mouth and mumbled something that Kayano could not make out.

"I beg your forgiveness, but I could not understand what you said, Ohishi."

"It is of no importance now, Kayano, of no importance—Let me tell you what has taken place in your absence. As you know, I summoned all the retainers of the castle to a meeting and informed them of the whole affair. After this, we discussed how everyone should commit seppuku, but they could not agree and started arguing among themselves. So I have decided to hold the castle to the last man against the government officers when they come to confiscate our lord's belongings. I have decided to divide our lord's war funds amongst his Samurai." To this Ohishi reached in his kimono and handed Kayano his share of remaining money.

But instead of Kayano taking the money, he hit Ohishi's hand, scattering the coins about the garden path. Ohishi jumped back, startled, "What is the meaning of this? Do you not wish to die here in honor, defending your lord's castle against the oncoming government officials?"

"Die! Die! You speak to me of dying. When I was ready to die by your own hand just a few days ago for letting our lord and clan down? But now you talk of dying here and letting our lord's killer go free. No, I am not afraid of dying, but let it be with a purpose. Let me die under the sword of my lord's enemy, not here by some government agent with whom I have no quarrel."

Ohishi reached out his hand and took Kayano by the arm, "My loyal friend, please let me explain. I am afraid I have not been completely truthful with you." There was a slight pause.

"What you do not know," Ohishi continued, "is that after I passed out the war funds, many of the so-called Samurai of our lord ran away and there are only sixty of us left. Now that I know your true feelings, there are sixty-one. Am I not right Kayano?"

Kayano could not help showing his delight. He smiled broadly. He leaped in the air and then quickly turned to Ohishi and said, "When do we strike? Tonight? Tomorrow? When, Ohishi? Tell me quickly."

"Not so fast my good friend," Ohishi replied. "Let us go into the courtyard where the rest are waiting and I will reveal to you my plan."

As all the retainers gathered in the courtyard, Ohishi Kuranosuke began to unfold his well-kept secret of how they would revenge their lord and kill Kira Kozuke-no-Suke. They each swore oaths of secrecy and pledged their lives to the fulfillment of their assigned tasks. They all agreed to surrender the castle and then disperse to become ronin.

Now Kira Kozuke-no-Suke was so sure that Ako Castle Samurai would attack him that he took every precaution and sent spies to watch the retainers' every move. But when they reported back to Kozuke-no-Suke that all the retainers had left the castle and had taken to the countryside to become ronin, he flew into a rage. "What do you mean," he stormed, "ronin! Do they think I am so stupid that I cannot see into this foolish plan? Now go and find and watch them,

Dokyo-Shoju holding off the ronin with ease

listen to everything that they say, and do not come back here until you find out their plans. Now get out of my sight until you have some information." At this he threw down his cup of tea and left the room.

As he entered the adjoining room, he summoned Dokyo Shoju, one of his most trusted retainers. When he saw Dokyo enter the room he quickly motioned to him to come to his side. Sake was prepared for them. Looking around to make sure they were alone, Kozuke-no-Suke began to pour sake and, speaking in a soft voice so that no one else could hear, he said, "Dokyo, I am sure that Asano's head Samurai, Ohishi Kuranosuke, will be the guiding light behind the attack against me, so it is most important that you find him and keep me posted on his every move. We cannot be too careful until this whole matter is settled." Talking hold of Dokyo's arm and looking into his eyes, he asked, "Do you understand, my good friend, just how important this mission is?" "Yes, my lord," Dokyo replied. "I will leave this very evening, and do not worry if Ohishi-san is planning an attack of any kind. I will discover it, and we will be ready. With this they lifted their sake cups and Dokyo departed.

For his own safety, because he expected treachery, Ohishi knew that he had to leave Ako as soon as possible, for if anything happened to him, his plan would never bear fruit. He packed his things, took his wife and children, and headed for Yamashina, a village east of Kyoto, capital of Japan.

Arriving in Yamashina, Ohishi purchased a house and land to make everyone think he had intentions of staying permanently. One day while he was working in his bonsai garden, he received word that Fuwa Kazuemon had married the daughter of the architect of Kira Kozuke-no-Suke's house and that the ronin now had the complete layout of every room in their enemy's dwelling. At this Ohishi was delighted, but there was disturbing news in that Kozuke-no-Suke was still protected by his father-in-law's Samurai and had sent Dokyo Shoju, his most trusted retainer, to spy on him.

Ohishi sat down on a rock in his garden and began to ponder. "So this old fox is still watching and listening to my every move. Good, it could not be better. For what Kozuke-no-Suke did not know was that many of the ronin had separated from their families and had gone out into the world as tradesmen or artisans and had also distinguished themselves in the occupations so that it was easier for them to gain entry to his mansion. They, of course, were spying. Ohishi knew too, that several of his retainers had left the league one by one until there were only forty-seven men left to carry out his plan. But this would be enough to do what had to be done. The most important thing now was to keep Kozuke-no-Suke completely off-guard.

Ohishi, determined to throw the enemy completely off his trail of revenge, started living a life of apparent despair. It became a common thing to see Ohishi in the brothels of Kyoto or Osaka, drunk and behaving badly. One evening after he returned from one of these outings, Ohishi's wife pleaded with him, "Ohishi, my beloved husband, please! You must stop this drunkenness; it is ruining our lives and there is little money left to live on. I understand your plan, but you have gone too far. We cannot live like this!"

"We?" Ohishi shouted, "We cannot live like this? Well, we do not have to! Get out! Get out and stay out. Take the children too! I do not want to see any of you here again!"

"You cannot mean this! Ohishi-san," his wife begged, "Please do not send us away. I am sorry for having said these things. Please let us stay."

But Ohishi's mind was made up, though his heart was broken, for he loved his wife and children. It had to be done, he thought. It would be much better for everyone; the family would be safe away from here. After his family had left Yamashina, Ohishi brought a woman by the name of Okanu to his house to become his mistress. Okanu was known throughout Kyoto for her beauty and pleasing manners and knew nothing of Ohishi's plot of revenge. One night when Ohishi was returning home drunk, he stumbled and fell flat on his back in the street. While he was trying to rise on one knee, a Samurai who knew Ohishi happened by. He stopped and looking down upon him, proclaimed in a loud voice so that others stopped and started to laugh, "Is this the great Samurai Ohishi Kuranosuke, head retainer of my beloved friend, Lord Asano Takumi-no-Kami? No! This cannot be him, for the Ohishi-san I knew would be too busy revenging his lord's death instead of lying about in the street, drunk."

To this Ohishi said nothing but reached out his hand for help. Instead, the Samurai lifted his foot and placing it on Ohishi's left shoulder, gave him a hardy push. Ohishi fell backwards. "This is indeed where you belong," the Samurai proclaimed and spit upon him.

When Dokyo Shoju heard of the incident, he reported back to Kozuke-no-Suke immediately. They were convinced that the Ako clan would do nothing, that there was not a true Samurai amongst them. No Samurai of any class would have permitted someone to spit upon him without killing the offender on the spot, even if it took the last ounce of life in his body. So with this news Kozuke-no-Suke felt more secure and returned half of the borrowed guards to his father-in-law. He did however, feel that it would be wise for his spies to keep their ears and eyes open as a precaution. Eventually, they grew weary of watching and became less interested in the ronin's movements.

When Ohishi heard what his enemy had done and that Dokyo had stayed in Edo with his lord, he knew that the time was at hand. Now that he was not watched so closely, he slipped out and went to Osaka. There he had a meeting with his old friend Amanoya Rihei, a merchant. He supplied Ohishi with all the weapons that would be needed to carry out his plan of revenge. After returning home Ohishi sent word for all forty-six men to meet just outside of Edo at a place they had previously agreed upon.

It was January 19, 1702 when the last man, Kayano, came through the small door to where the rest were waiting. Ohishi could not help but feel delight when he saw his old friend bowing to him. He motioned for Kayano to join the rest. Ohishi began to speak, "My fellow retainers, we have long awaited this moment. There is no need to speak of the hardships we have all endured, because that is all in the past. Now we must look to the plan of revenging our lord." As Ohishi looked around the room he motioned to Nakamiya Kansuke, "Did you bring the plans of Kozuke-no-Suke's home?" Nakamiya handed them to Ohishi. He had made two sets and everyone gathered around eagerly.

Ohishi resumed, "Very well, my loyal friends. Chiba here has informed me that our enemy is going to give a tea party tomorrow night, so we know that he will be home. Tomorrow night after the party, when everyone is asleep, we will strike. If you were not able to bring your weapons, take one of these and make yourself ready."

As Ohishi handed out the weapons, he proclaimed, "Do not forget to write your documents explaining who we are and what we are going to do. We do not want to be mistaken for bandits."

He then divided the group into two parties to study the house plans. "This is my plan. As you can see by the drawings, we must be very careful not to let anyone escape through the rear. They might bring reinforcements from Kozuke-no-Suke's father-in-law. We do not want any more bloodshed than is necessary.

About half an hour before the attack, I want you, Hara-san and Fuwa-san, to go tell all of Kozuke-no-Suke's neighbors what we are planning to do; this will keep them from worrying about being attacked too. I do not think we have anything to worry about from them, because as my reports indicate, they all dislike him as much as we do. We will divide ourselves into three groups. I will take one and my son will take another. The third will be made up of eight men. These eight men will be stationed on the walls." Ohishi pointed at the map, "Here, here, here and there. The other four will be stationed here and here, so they can see anyone who might try and escape using the front or back gates. It will be their duty to make sure that no one escapes. These eight will be our best archers. My group will come in through the front gate, here. The other group will enter through this fourth back gate on the west side, there. The signal will be the beating of the drum in the Yamaya Soko manner. We probably will not receive much resistance until we get to this point; the courtyard to the main house. But no matter, we must push through until the two groups join together, here. If anyone should find Kozuke-no-Suke before I do, blow your whistle. Do not kill him until we can be sure it is he and we can all be there to witness the act. Are there any questions?" Ohishi slowly looked around the room but no one spoke. He smiled, and getting up from the box on which he was sitting, opened it. "Good," he said, "then let us all have a last drink together." He picked up two sake bottles.

Early the following morning, at two o'clock, all the retainers began to gather and by 2:30 everything was ready for their long-awaited attack. Snow was falling heavily by the time the small band reached Kozuke-no-Suke's mansion. Ohishi motioned for everyone to gather around him and speaking in a low tone, he addressed Hara. "We will give you thirty minutes, no longer, to awaken the neighbors and inform them. Everyone else is to go to their stations. Remember if the household should awake before I have sounded the attack, proceed as planned. With this bright clear moon, we should have no problems. Kill only when necessary. Dispatch only those who offer resistance." He pulled his katana from its resting place and waved it high in the air. "We must not fail!" he vowed, and the small band began to disperse through the heavy snow.

The minutes seemed like hours as the ronin awaited the signal, and though it was bitterly cold, no one seemed to feel it. All at once the attack sound broke the silence of the night and inspired the retainers with inexplicable courage. Kayano was the first man to reach the guardhouse at the gate. With swords in hands, he slid the door open quietly with a foot. The men pushed past him. He then quickly stepped inside. Taking his short sword and lightly poking it at the blanket laying on the floor and with his long sword raised above his head in a ready position, he spoke, "Give us the keys to the gate and no harm will come to you." The man, half asleep, rose on one elbow, "What is going on here?" "Give us the keys to the gate," Kayano replied, this time pushing at the man a little harder with his sword. "I do not have them," answered the man in a shaky voice. The other ronin were standing with their swords pointed at the other two guards, watching every move. "We have no time to argue with you," Kayano said, "We are here to revenge our lord, Asano Takumi-no-Kami." Before he could continue, the guard reached for his katana resting in its rack. But he was far too slow and his severed arm fell to the floor. His loud cry of pain was silenced by Kayano's second cut across the neck. Kayano turned to the other two guards. "Well, what about you? I suppose that you know nothing about the keys either," he surmised, while shaking the blood from his sword. "Never mind, tie them up. We will break down the gate." Returning the short sword to its saya, he turned and left the room.

In the few short minutes that passed, Kayano could hear the cries of battle on the other side of the wall. "Hurry up in there," he commanded. "We do not want to be the last to arrive at the main house." Once past the gate, Kayano's group broke up into several smaller groups. The fighting was spreading throughout the compound. As Kayano turned a corner, he found himself facing two of Kozuke-no-Suke's Samurai. Quickly pulling his short sword, he charged straight forward. The surprising suddenness of his charge allowed him to cut one of the Samurai in half. But as he turned to face the other, he slipped in the pool of blood, landing on his back. Immediately the Samurai attacked with an overhead swing of his blade. Kayano could see the sword coming down threatening to deprive him of his sworn revenge. Taking hold of the upper torso of the dead Samurai lying beside him, he pulled it atop himself as a shield. The blade struck, and though he feared the blade might cut through the impromptu shield, the body held. As the Samurai prepared for his second cut, Kayano grabbed a handful of blood and sand and flung it into his attacker's face. Rolling to his side, he made a low horizontal cut dividing the attacker from his front foot. Jumping to his feet, he finished off the Samurai with a second cut and ran to the courtyard of the main house.

When Kayno arrived in the courtyard, he discovered small duels of two and three men everywhere. One battle caught his eye. On the porch of the main house, Kozuke-no-Suke's head retainer, Dokyo Shoju, had three of the ronin fighting for their lives. He was astounded. Dokyo was fighting like a mad man, but using his swords with such ease, parrying and countering each attack as though it were child's play. The ronin were slowly being driven back off the porch. This enraged Kayano. He commanded at the top of his voice, "Stop this retreating at once! You made a vow to give up your life to revenge our lord's death and yet you back away from death as if there were a choice." The words cut through the falling snow like an icy wind and taking hold of the ronin, pushed them forward. It was not long before they had pushed Dokyo back up the steps. He was now fighting for the inches of ground on which he stood. Finally, Kayano picked up a lance and threw it between the ronin, hitting Dokyo in the neck. As they watched, Dokyo dropped his short sword, grabbing hold of the lance, trying desperately to remove it from his neck. He swung wildly with the katana in his other hand. For a moment, Kayano feared Dokyo might yet kill the ronin with his fierce persistence in living. Then, as when a light breeze causes the cherry blossoms to fall from the tree, Dokyo fell forward, down the steps, dead at the ronin's feet.

Kayano thought to himself how brave a Samurai they had slain! But his thoughts were quickly broken off by Ohishi's voice, "Over here Kayano, quickly! Kayano ran quickly to Ohishi's side where most of the other ronin had already gathered. Ohishi raised his sword in the air. "We have won," he shouted, "but what good is this victory if Kozuke-no-Suke has escaped. He cannot be found anywhere," Ohishi said, circling his sword to encompass the estate. "Spread out and search again. If he is not found, we will meet here and commit seppuku. Now go, and let not this battle have been fought in vain!" Looking at Kayano, Ohishi pointed at the main gate, "We will look again in there." They reached Kozuke-no-Suke's sleeping quarters but still without a clue to their enemy's whereabouts. Suddenly Kayano shouted excitedly, "It is warm! I tell you, it is warm! Here, feel this blanket; I tell you it is still warm." Ohishi gave a signal and the ronin came running from every direction to the sleeping quarters.

"Kozuke-no-Suke is not far from this very spot," Ohishi shouted. "Look everywhere, tear up the floors and ceilings if necessary, but find him!" There was now new hope for the ronin and they tore the room apart in their search. Moments later Muramatsu Kihei shouted to the others, "Look here, behind this silk screen on the wall. There is a hole big enough for a man to crawl through!" Muramatsu took his sword and ran it deep into the cavity, but to no avail. He then crept inside the small tunnel probing ahead with his sword. After sliding along on his hands and knees for about 10 feet, he came to an opening that led into a small courtyard. Still there was no sign of Kozuke-no-Suke. The other ronin started pouring out of the tunnel into the courtyard. Muramatsu spotted a small woodshed in the far corner and approached it, shouting "Kozuke-no-Suke, come out! I, Muramatsu Kihei Hidenao, ronin of Ako, know of your cowardice in fleeing, but now you have been found. I demand that you come out and meet your responsibilities!"

There was no response from inside the small shed. Before Muramatsu could say another word, Kayano pushed him to one side, kicked in the door and began to stab savagely into the darkness with his katana. There came a loud cry of pain and Kayano emerged with blood dripping from his sword onto the white snow. "Drag him out where we can see him for the coward that he is!" Kayano exclaimed. Two ronin complied, dragging an elderly man dressed in white sleeping dress from the darkness of the shed. As Kayano raised his sword to put an end to the old man's life, Ohishi shouted, "Stop, you have half killed him already," pointing to a large cut on the old man's side. "We are not animals," Ohishi continued. Taking the old man by the arm, he led him to the center of the small courtyard and asked Muramatsu to fetch a lantern so they might make sure that this was truly Kozuke-no-Suke.

As the small band of brave ronin gathered about, Muramatsu returned with a small but adequate light. Holding it in front of their prisoner, Ohishi grabbed the old man's topknot and held his face to the light in the falling snow. "Can anyone identify this man as Kozuke-no-Suke, killer of our lord, Asano Takumino-Kami?"

Silence followed and a gust of wind blew the snow in frigid eddies about the courtyard. Then Kayano shoved aside several of the ronin. "I know this man to be Kozuke-no-Sake. I say let us waste no more time! Cut off his head and let us be on our way." "All in good time, Kayano," Ohishi said, reaching into his kimono. He withdrew a small tanto and handed it to the old man.

"We were the retainers of our departed lord, Asano Takumi-no-Kami, who came to you last year for instruction. Because of the evil in your heart, he was forced to die by his own hand. We now demand that you commit seppuku with this same tanto, which our lord himself used in his own ceremony."

The old man dropped the knife in the snow and leaning away from it, began to beg for his life. Ohishi tried desperately to persuade him to kill himself with honor, but to no avail. Seeing that the man was hysterical and that any further persuasion was useless, Ohishi picked up the small knife and motioned to Kayano and Muramatsu to hold the old man's arms and head down. Kozuke-no-Suke began to scream and beg for his life at the top of his voice; but none of the ronin listened to his pleas. Ohishi, removing the saya from the small knife, proclaimed for everyone to hear, "I take the head of our sworn enemy—Kozuke-no-Suke—in the name of our beloved lord, Asano-no-Kami."

In a moment, the cries for mercy were silenced. The head was then wrapped in a cloth and placed in a bucket. The small band marched out of the courtyard carrying the bucket. The snow had stopped. No words were exchanged between the ronin as they filed out but when Kayano reached the small gate, he could not help but look back at the headless body, thrashing about as a fish out of water, thinking to himself that justice had finally been served. "Now at last I will be able to meet my lord eye to eye," he thought.

It was now nearly six o'clock in the morning. The attack had lasted about two hours and to the surprise of Ohishi, they had not lost a single man. As the band of ronin marched in pride, carrying their trophy in the bucket, the word of the attack spread like fire. Soon people began to cheer them along the roadside as they passed. They arrived at the temple of Sengakuji, their lord's burial place south of Yedo, by mid-morning. After they reported their deeds and intentions to the head priest, they carefully washed the bloody head in a well outside of the temple grounds and then proceeded to their lord's grave. Ohishi gathered everyone about the grave and reported in a loud voice as though their master were still alive, all the circumstances of the revenge.

The ronin washing Kozuke's head

When the ceremony was concluded, the small band gave themselves up to government officials. The date for the execution of their sentence was January 24, 1702. The courts divided the small band into three groups: seventeen were turned over to Kosokawa Etchu-no-Kami, Lord of Chofu, and twenty were turned over to Okino-Kami, Lord of Matsuyama. The rest were sent to Mizuno Kenmatsu, Lord of Okazaki. The total number of ronin taken in charge by the daimyo was forty-seven. On the tenth of March, 1703, they were ordered to commit seppuku in succession in the mansions of the respective daimyo that had them in his charge. They were buried at Sengakuji Temple beside the tomb of their beloved lord, whom they had served so well.

You may ask, after counting the tombstones, "There are forty-eight stones. Who is the other one?" Here we have a true Samurai also—one who carried the code of Bushido to the end along with the ronin. His name was Bukko Takuan. He came to the grave site one summer morning and standing before Ohishi Kuranosuke's grave, proclaimed, "I, Bukko Takuan, who knew not of the plot of revenge you carried in your heart last year and who kicked and spit upon you causing you more disgrace than I can bear, do hereby beg your forgiveness." After which he took a small dirk from his obi and stabbed himself until he was dead. The priest of the temple, knowing of his grief and wishing to comfort his spirit, buried him beside the ronin.

Even today people still flock to visit the graves and pray for these fearless men. The Japanese people will never forget the memory of these faithful and valiant clansmen. Once every sixty years, the priests hold a two-month festival commemorating the deeds of the Loyal Forty-Seven Ronin.

The farewell testimony of Yoshio Oishi (ronin)

The graves as they are arranged in the temple

The Tomb of the 47 Loyal Retainers at Sehgakuji Temple—Tokyo, Japan

The grave site

The entrance to the grave site

Yoroi (A set of armor worn by one of the 47 ronin on exhibit in the temple's museum)

A headstone in the graveyard—the slash at the top of the name indicates that the ronin committed seppuku

References

D. T. Suzuki, *Essays in Zen Buddhism, Third Series.* New York: Samuel Weiser Inc., p. 144

D. T. Suzuki, *Zen and Japanese Culture.* Princeton, NJ: Princeton University Press, 1971

W. D. Jennings, *The Ronin.* Rutland, VT: Charles E. Tuttle Co., 1968. p. 129

Rodger Fitlock, "Japanese Cross," *Black Belt Magazine*, Vol. 7, Number 5, May 1969. p. 49

B. W. Robinson, *The Arts of the Japanese Sword*, Rutland, VT: Charles E. Tuttle Co., 1971. p. 15

Donn F. Draeger, *Asian Fighting Arts.* New York: Berkley Publishing Corp. p. 101

A. B. Mitford (Lord Redesdale), *Tales of Old Japan,* "Appendix A: An Account of the Hara-Kiri." Rutland, VT: Charles E. Tuttle Co., 1970

Van de Wetering J., *The Empty Mirror*, Boston, The Houghton Mifflin Company, 1974

Eugene Herrigel, *Zen in the Art of Archery.* New York: Bantheon Books, 1953

Shunryu Suzuki, *Zen Mind, Beginner's Mind.* New York: John Weatherhill, Inc., 1974. p. 21

Glossary

AIKUCHI: dagger without a tsuba

ASHI: foot

BUJUTSU: working parts of Iaido

BUSHI: old term for Samurai

CHIBURI: removing blood from the sword

CHING: limits

CHUDAN: center readiness with the sword

DAISHO: two matched swords

DATTO: removing the katana from obi

DIRK: small knife used in seppuku

DO: way

DOJO: school or training hall

EDO: old name for Tokyo

EMBU: practice of martial arts

HA: cutting edge of a sword

HAKAMA: Samurai's divided skirt

HANSHI: Iai master

HAPPO-GIRI: style of eight cutting directions

HAPPO-NO-KAMAE: style of eight directions

HARAI-GOSHI: hip throw

HARA-KIRI: everyday word used for abdomen cutting

HASSO: ready position with the sword tsuba even with your chin

HENOBE: formal Samurai dress

HEYAZASHI: small dagger

HOJO JINSUKE: said to be the founder of Iai in 1600

IAI: drawing the sword

IAI-GOSHI: letting the waist sink

IAI-HIZA: sitting with raised knee

JODAN: overhead position with the sword

JUTSU: art-method or technique

KAISHAKU: second in seppuku

KAMI-NO-ASHI: upper foot nearest the shrine

KAMIZA: place of honor in a dojo

KARASUGUCHI: crow beak crack at the top of a sword

KATA: form of practice

KATANA: long sword

KENDO: sword way

KENSEI: sword saint

KESAGIRI: scapular cut with a sword

KIRITSUKE: cutting

KISSAKI: tip of a sword

KIZU: flaws on a sword

KODOGU: hardware on a sword

KOJIRI cap on the end of a saya

KOSHI-ITA: stiffener in the back of a hakama

KYOSHI: one rank below hanshi

MAI: inscription on a tang

MEIJI: period spanning the late nineteenth and early twentieth centuries in Japan

MEN: head

MENUI: ornament in a sword handle

MORI-RYU: a style of Iaido

MOROTE-SUKI: two-handed thrust

MU-GAI-RYU: style of Iai-Jitsu

MUNE: back side of a sword, 8 inches from the tip

MUNEN: to have no thought

MURAMASA: famed sword maker

MUSASHI, MIYAMOTO: famed Samurai and expert swordsman (1584–1645)

MUSHIN: to have an empty mind

MYOYO: spiritual attainment

Noto: returning a sword to saya
Nukikata: drawing the sword
Nukitsuke: the draw
Obi: belt
Rei: formal bow
Ronin: masterless knight or Samurai
Ryu: style
Sageo: cord on the saya
Saineikan: Imperial Palace dojo
Samurai: knight or soldier of Japan
Sanpogiri: three-way cut
Saya: scabbard
Sayabiki: pulling the saya to meet the sword guard
Seiza: sitting in place
Sensei: teacher
Seppuku: formal word used for abdomen cutting
Shinogj: back side of a sword
Shinza: shinto altar
Shinzen: a Shinto term meaning "before a god"
Shogun: war lord
Sonkyo: sitting on the balls of the feet
Tachi: slung sword
Taijo: procedure of leaving the practice area
Taito Shisei: standing with the sword in the belt

Tanden: abdomen center of power
Tang: part of the blade that extends into the handle
Tanto: dagger
Te: hand
Teito Shisei: formal standing
Tomoe: circle
Torei: formal bow to the sword
Tow: defender in a kata
Tsuba: sword guard
Tsuka: handle of the sword
Tsuka-ate: striking with end of a sword handle
Tsukagashira: end of a sword handle
Tsukahara Bokuden: famed swordsman (1490–1572)
Uchiko: limestone powder fo cleaning swords
Ukenagashi: warding off ar attack
Ushiro: behind
Wakizashi: short sword
Waza: technique
Ya: attacker in a kata
Yakiba: temper line on sword
Yoko: side
Zen: A Buddhist sect
Zanshin: spiritual pr paration

"Books to Span the East and West"

Tuttle Publishing was founded in 1832 in the small New England town of Rutland, Vermont [USA]. Our core values remain as strong today as they were then—to publish best-in-class books which bring people together one page at a time. In 1948, we established a publishing office in Japan—and Tuttle is now a leader in publishing English-language books about the arts, languages and cultures of Asia. The world has become a much smaller place today and Asia's economic and cultural influence has grown. Yet the need for meaningful dialogue and information about this diverse region has never been greater. Over the past seven decades, Tuttle has published thousands of books on subjects ranging from martial arts and paper crafts to language learning and literature—and our talented authors, illustrators, designers and photographers have won many prestigious awards. We welcome you to explore the wealth of information available on Asia at **www.tuttlepublishing.com**.